DELINQUENCY
TOLERANCE

DELINQUENCY TOLERANCE

JUVENILE APPETITE FOR CRIMINAL BEHAVIOR

EVARISTUS OBINYAN

Outskirts Press, Inc.
Denver, Colorado

Keywords:

Delinquency, Tolerance, Pharmaco-Social Friction, Juvenile, Adolescence

٢٢٢

A research effort into a previously uninhabited terrain in criminological literature can be a daunting project. This dissertation presents an account of such a study. This project could not have been accomplished without the intensive counsel and direct assistance of my major professor and members of my Dissertation committee.

I am absolutely proud of the distinguished members of my committee whose wisdom and superior academic experience help propel the success of my graduate program.

I am particularly and deeply indebted to Dr. Michael Lynch, my advisor and major professor, whose countless hours of consistent advisement and encouragement throughout the course of my studies greatly imparted the completion of my project. Dr. Lynch's wealth of knowledge and experience in the field of criminology was tapped throughout the study. I want to thank Dr. Wilson Palacios for his contribution and advisements. Dr. Dwayne Smith, the department head made an essential contribution by allowing me access to complete this program in the department of criminology. I want to thank Dr. Susan Fogel for reading the manuscripts and Dr. Cochran and Dr. Miekowski for their respective assistance.

My sincere appreciation is extended to the department of criminology and the University of South Florida, which has given me a renewed respect for academia.

I wish to acknowledge Lisa Landis, student advisor for her patience with me especially during registration. I must thank sincerely Leon County Schools for access to survey participants during the investigation. Finally, I want to thank my family for their support. What a Journey?

Table of Contents

List of Tables

Abstract

The study was designed to examine the attitudes of adolescents towards the tolerance of delinquent behavior. It was postulated that there would be a differential in the tolerance of delinquent behavior by juveniles from different age, gender, and racial groups. It was hypothesized that different groups would score higher or lower on select measures or dimensions (definition, reporting, controlling, preventing, correcting) of delinquency tolerance, and that their level of tolerance of delinquency might prove useful in explaining participation in delinquency.

The focus of the study was on identification of differential attitudes of various subgroups towards the violations of norms relating to acceptable behavior by adolescents. Definition and reporting dimensions are crucial index of tolerance attitudes towards delinquency.

The study design employed an in-school opinion survey. The total survey sample was 562 county school students from elementary, middle and high schools. Participation was voluntary. Parents had to provide consent slips in order for their children to participate. Teachers were given the option of having their class participate. As a result of these survey techniques, the sample was non-random. The characteristics of the sample population and county population for these age groups, however, were similar.

The major hypothesis of the study was that there is differential tolerance of delinquency amongst juveniles of different race and gender groups. This hypothesis was confirmed. Important significant difference for gender (males were more tolerant of delinquency than females) and ethnicity (Asian were less tolerant of delinquency than blacks, whites or Hispanics) and Blacks were more tolerant of delinquency than are Whites.

The significance of this research is its potential impact on theoretical explanations of delinquency. The implications of these results for revising existing theories of delinquency are discussed in the concluding chapter.

Introduction

The Purpose of the Study

This is and examination of differential adolescent tolerance of delinquent behavior by juvenile/adolescent race and gender group. It has been hypothesized that adult criminal behavior is affected by tolerance of crime. Two studies have examined this hypothesis and found some support for this view. The impact of juvenile tolerance on delinquency has not, however, been examined, and this study marks the first known effort to assess whether this idea may be useful for explaining juvenile delinquency.

Juveniles who tolerate crime express attitudes that accept criminal behavior. In addition, youth who tolerate delinquency may reject criminal behavior as unacceptable, but fail to act to prevent acts they view as unacceptable when faced with such behavior.

This study employs a survey to ask youth about their attitudes toward several different delinquent acts, and how they would react if they witnessed others who engaged in those acts. Why ask adolescents about their tolerance of delinquency? To understand how youths are feeling about crime and victimization, to find out what they are thinking and feeling about their lives, the world around them and their tolerance of delinquency, and, most importantly, to discover whether tolerance of delinquency is constant or variable across race and gender groups. The author believes that by examining adolescent tolerance of delinquency, we can begin to explore whether youth are becoming desensitized to crime, and whether this is associated with higher levels of criminal participation. This study is designed to find answers to pertinent questions about youths' attitudes toward tolerance of delinquent and / or criminal behavior.

Adolescent attitudes regarding the definition, reporting, controlling, preventing, and correcting of delinquent and / or criminal behavior will be examined as part of the investigation of tolerance of delinquency. It is hope that such an investigation yields information that helps to explain participation in delinquent acts.

Two important facts are known about delinquent behavior: rates of delinquency are higher among boys than girls, and among African-Americans compared to whites. Thus, it is important to test the idea of tolerance against what is know about the association between gender, race and delinquency. For tolerance to be a useful explanation, it should vary across race and gender groups and explain the race-delinquency and gender-delinquency patterns noted in prior research.

Numerous studies have examined the nature of, trends in, and the distribution and causes of juvenile delinquency in the United States. Despite this extensive literature, the United States appears to be no closer to solving the problem of juvenile delinquency than it was fifty years ago when delinquency research first became a significant area of academic interest. How can this lack of progress related to controlling delinquency be explained? Three broad explanations are relevant.

First, it is possible that the delinquency control policies are inconsistent with research findings, and fail to adequately address the known causes and correlates of delinquency. Second, it is also possible that existing theoretical explanations that inform policy are not useful explanations of delinquency. As a result, previously implemented policies have failed to address the causes of delinquency because the theories they are based on are inaccurate. Third, the continued problem of delinquency may be the result of a combination of both inappropriate theory and policy.

Beginning with these observations, the purpose of this dissertation is to examine an alternative explanation for delinquency that also possesses the ability to inform policies for delinquency reduction. To achieve this goal, this dissertation examines the relationship between tolerance of delinquency by youths and the potential impact tolerance may have on engaging in delinquent acts. To address policy issues, this dissertation ties youths' tolerance of delinquency to Emile Durkheim's discussion of the role the secular state should play in the socialization of youth in his book, *Moral Education*. Durkheim's work is important to an analysis of tolerance because it was here that Durkheim described the how secular socialization mechanisms should be used to educate children about acceptable social values. Theoretically, if society could establish an acceptable tolerance threshold, it would make youth uncomfortable with the idea that delinquency is an acceptable form of behavior. Determining how this could be accomplished was the major goal of Durkheim's work.

Little previous research has been conducted on the issue of tolerance of criminal or delinquent behavior. In fact, no previous research has examined the issue of tolerance of delinquency by juveniles to any extent. For example, Faust (1970) examined *adult tolerance* of juvenile delinquency. In a later study, Sharp (1983) examined one aspect of delinquency tolerance by juveniles, and consequently is of limited usefulness for understanding this issue. As a result, those seeking to perform a study focusing on tolerance of delinquency by juveniles are provided with little guidance in extant literature.

In a review of previous studies on delinquency, Barri Flowers (1990) lamented the lack of empirical studies addressing juveniles' views on delinquency. While studies involving adults' attitudes toward a variety of crime and justice issues are widely found in the criminological literature, the juvenile subject's attitudes toward crime and punishment remains absent. In such an intellectual environment, it remains difficult to understand whether juveniles and adults share views about crime and justice, whether these views affect participation in crime, and the extent to which juvenile and adult tolerance of crime correspond or diverge. From the perspective of this study, it is difficult to understand if youths' tolerance of delinquency plays a role in the creation of delinquent behaviors given the lack of data on juveniles' tolerance of delinquency.

But, what exactly is tolerance? A full discussion of this term is found in chapter 2. Here, however, it is necessary to provide at least some idea of what the term tolerance means.

In a broad sense, tolerance consists of two components: an attitudinal component and a behavioral component. Both measure the extent to which an individual is willing to accept an idea, behavior, event or even other kinds of people. The attitudinal component of tolerance of delinquency, for example, consists of youths' definitions of specific acts of delinquency as acceptable or unacceptable. But, to determine whether an individual tolerates something, we must know more than their attitude toward that thing; we must also know how they would act or behave in its presence. In the case of tolerance of delinquency, the behavioral measure is represented by examining whether juveniles believe that they would report a delinquent act they witness, and by measuring how they believe society should respond to delinquent acts.

Why is it important to measure both the attitudinal and behavioral dimensions of tolerance of delinquency? It is possible, for example, for youth to assert that stealing is unacceptable behavior. When faced with a situation where they are confronted with someone who steals, however, the question is do they act on their tolerance attitude, or do they fail to act. Acting in ways consistent with attitudes tells us that the youth has a well developed sense of intolerance toward delinquency, while failure to act indicates that youth are more tolerant of delinquency than their attitudes towards delinquent behaviors would indicate. In other words, we can only determine if youth tolerate delinquency by knowing about both their attitudes and actions.

Before proceeding, it should be made clear that this dissertation constitutes an initial investigation into the utility of the concept of tolerance as an explanation for delinquency. This focus affected the type of data collected. The data for this study involve youths' attitudes toward definitions, and the reporting and control of delinquent acts. These data are needed to determine whether or not youth tolerate delinquency. It is not the purpose of this dissertation, however, to test whether youth who tolerate delinquency are more or less likely than youth who do not tolerate delinquency to engage in delinquent acts. Such a study should only be undertaken after the first premise on tolerance has been examined, and data indicate that further development of this view is warranted. Nevertheless, some hypotheses concerning how tolerance of delinquency might affect participation in delinquency are offered to examine the utility of this view.

Background

Three persistent findings concerning the correlates of delinquency stand out in previous research. These findings suggest that participation in delinquency is related to age, race/ethnicity and gender of youth. Older youth, minorities and males have consistently higher rates of delinquency than younger youth, non-minorities and females. Thus, from both a theoretical and policy position it makes sense to explain how these factors relate to delinquency, and to the policies that could be implemented to reduce the relationship between these factors and participation in delinquency.

Consistent with previous findings, this dissertation will

emphasize how and why tolerance of delinquency varies with race/ethnicity and gender. This is an important consideration because the failure of tolerance to vary along gender and race/ethnic lines would imply that the concept of tolerance is not useful for explaining participation in delinquency.

As noted, delinquency tolerance (or tolerance or delinquency) measures youths' attitudes toward the appropriateness of definitions of, the reporting of and state responses to delinquency. Thus, the first dimension of delinquency tolerance is called "defining." In order to study delinquency tolerance among youth, we must first discover how they define delinquency, and whether youth share a common definition of delinquency. We are interested in youths' definitions of delinquency is for two reasons. First, youths' attitudes toward the defining of delinquency are examine to determine whether youth perceive delinquency as wrong. This attitude helps measure whether youth tolerate the existence of this form of deviance attitudinally. Second, we wish to discover whether youths' tolerance of delinquency varies with race/ethnic and gender correlates of delinquency. Variations along these dimensions are expected to conform to know levels of delinquency offending if the theory of tolerance is to be judged as a useful explanation of delinquency.

The second dimension of tolerance of delinquency is called "reporting." In order to study youths' tolerance of delinquency, we must not only know how they define delinquency, but whether they will act on their perceptions. For example, if youth define stealing as wrong, but indicate that they would not stop or report acts of stealing that they witness, then we can conclude that they are tolerant of this behavior. In contrast, where youth report disapprove of a behavior, and are willing to respond to that behavior, we can say that they are intolerant of delinquency. It is also plausible that youth who tolerate delinquency are more likely than youth who do not tolerate delinquency to engage in delinquent behavior themselves.

The third dimension of delinquency tolerance is composed of attitudes toward the correction, prevent and control of delinquency. Here, we are interested in discovering the association between youths' definitions of delinquency and their belief that society ought to do something about those acts. The more youth tolerate delinquency, the less likely they are to believe that society should respond formally to these acts.

Exposure to and Tolerance of Delinquency

Delinquency has been a persistent problem in American society. For example, it has been estimated that courts with juvenile jurisdiction handled 1,755,100 delinquency cases in 1997 (U.S. Bureau of Census, 1999). Between 1988 and 1997, the number of delinquency cases processed by U.S. juvenile courts increased by 48 percent (OJJDP Statistical Briefing Book, 2000). Over this time period, caseloads increased across the four major offense categories: personal crimes (+ 97%); property offenses (+19%), drug offenses (+125%), and public order offenses (+67%) (Butts and Snyder, 1997). Despite recent declines in official delinquency, the level of delinquency remains quite high.

Numerous theoretical perspectives have been suggested to explain the causes of delinquency. A number of approaches employ attitudinal measures to predict delinquency. Consistent with this emphasis, this dissertation examines attitudes that reflect tolerance of delinquency. Previous delinquency research has not, however, examined the issue of tolerance.

The examination of adolescent's attitudes toward delinquency or their tolerance of norm violations in different instances may help explain why the United States has such a high rate of delinquency. Following classical sociological reasoning, it is plausible that youths' tolerance of delinquency reflects the socialization process to which they have been exposed. There are several studies indicating that lack of parental supervision, which may enhance tolerance of delinquency, contributes to delinquency. Data from various agencies indicate that some of the factors associated with lack of parental supervision have been increasing or are significantly large. For example, Census Bureau figures indicate that the proportion of children living in single-parent homes more than doubled between 1970 and 1997--- from 12 to 28 percent (Snyder, 1999). Another family-related factor could be the lack of role models in single-parent families. OJJDP estimated that nearly 1 million American teenagers age 15 to 19 become pregnant each year, that approximately 3 in 10 children live in single-parent homes, and that the majority of these children (85%) lived with their mothers (Garry and Maynard, 1999).

Others suggest that the risk factors involved in youth violence are attributable to gang involvement, poor academic achievement, poverty, mental states, school dropouts, and alcohol or other substance abuses. These factors may also impact tolerance of delinquency. For example, some researcher suggests that youths who witness violent events may be cognitively affected by their observation of violence on both emotionally and developmentally levels, perhaps altering their tolerance of delinquent acts. As an example of the extent of this problem, a Chicago public school student- survey of 1000 inner-city youths in middle and high schools reported that 23 percent had witnessed someone being murdered (Chaiken, 2000). In a similar study, a survey taken from a police district with high homicide rates revealed that 45 percent of students had witnessed a killing (Ramus, 1995). Furthermore, a larger number of adolescents witness near-deadly violence (Ramus, 1995). In another study of low income, central city youths, 27 percent of those surveyed met the diagnostic criteria for posttraumatic stress disorder (PTSD) (Esbensen and Huizinga, 1993). The conclusion was that victimization and witnessing violence are strongly associated with PTSD, and that exposure to violence and victimization are also strongly associated with subsequent violence or delinquency.

Youth are exposed to other forms of violence that may impact how they perceive delinquency. Studies on "bullying" behavior, for example, (The National Institute of Child Health and Human Development; NICHD) found that a significant numbers of youth are victims of bullying on a daily basis. This study found that bullying has long-term and short-term psychological effects on both bullies and the bullied. The study indicates that the victims of such acts experience loneliness and reported having trouble making social and various emotional adjustments including insecurity, poor relationships, loss of self-esteem and even fear of attending school. Further, victims may carry the impact over to adulthood, and are at greater risk of suffering from depression and other mental health problems such as schizophrenia and suicide.

The mass media has made modern youth more aware of delinquent and violent behaviors, bombarding them with images of criminal acts through the movies, television and video games . In the past, adults or parents were better able to shield their children from these corrupting influences. Adults have increasingly exposed young people to violent vocabularies, violent behavior, guns, drug use, sex, sexual misconduct, and other immoral behavior (lies, obnoxious behavior, etc.) through the media (TV, internet, newspapers and magazine), at home, in the streets, and elsewhere. These various exposures to messages that legitimize deviance and crime may, for example, elevate youths' tolerance for these behaviors, lowering specific barriers to engaging in these or similar acts

In sum, evidence suggests that exposure to delinquency and violence impacts youth in numerous ways. One view suggests that this exposure desensitizes youth to violence and delinquency, and increases the probability that youth may resort to these behaviors. One reason youth may be more likely to resort to these behaviors is that their exposure to delinquency and violence increases their tolerance of these behaviors.

Conclusion

Delinquency has been a persistent problem in American society. Existing theory and policy have failed to provide a solution to this problem, suggesting the need to develop alternative explanations of delinquency.

This study contributes to this task by examining the concept of delinquency tolerance employing youths' attitudes toward the definition and reporting of delinquency. As a preliminary examination of this idea, this study is restricted to assessing whether tolerance of delinquency varies across youth, and does not directly measure whether youth who are more likely to engage in delinquency have a higher tolerance for delinquency.

Consistent with findings from previous research, the association between variations in age, race/ethnicity and gender of youth and their tolerance of delinquency will be examined. Theoretically, these correlates of delinquency should be associated with tolerance of delinquency to judge the merits of this approach to understanding delinquency.

Durkheim previously addressed the role of socialization in producing youth who would value widely held social beliefs. His position is consistent with theoretical issues connecting tolerance of delinquency to participating in delinquency through value socialization. Policies derived from Durkheim's view that may impact youths' tolerance of delinquency are also discussed.

CHAPTER 1 REVIEW QUESTIONS

1. Why should delinquency tolerance be studied?
2. Identify and discuss risk factors associated with delinquency tolerance
3. How can delinquency tolerance theory explain juvenile participation in crime?

Tolerance

This chapter examines the concept of tolerance. As a concept, tolerance has had many uses, and a long history. Traditionally, the word is defined in terms of recognizing and respecting others beliefs, practices, behaviors, etc., without necessarily agreeing with the meaning of their specific interpretation. As noted in the introductory chapter, in this dissertation, tolerance is defined as having two dimensions: attitudinal and behavioral. Someone who tolerates delinquency, for example, respects delinquent behavior as a choice others may make. This does not necessarily mean that they embrace delinquency; only that they recognize the right of others to freely choose deviance, as in the retributive tradition (Newman, 1985). In contrast, the person who does not tolerate delinquency disapproves of that behavior, and rejects the right of other to act in this way. In either case, however, the attitude a person expresses toward delinquency (tolerance or intolerance) represents only one dimension of their ability to tolerate delinquency. To determine whether an individual is truly tolerant of delinquency, however, we also need an indication of how that individual reacts, or how they indicate they would react to acts of delinquency. In other words, a person who is intolerant of delinquency would not only find that delinquency is "wrong," they would take some action against the delinquent.

The following review demonstrates that the concept of tolerance has both social and individual implications. On one hand, tolerance is a personal consideration or judgment that describes what a person is willing to accept or accommodate. Socially, collective levels of tolerance define the boundaries of diversity and difference a society is willing to accept and accommodate.

Historical Origins

The word tolerance was first used to describe attitudes and actions towards various religious and political groups. The angelic doctor, Thomas Aquinas (Summa Theologiae) wrote the first major work that discusses tolerance or toleration by name. Examining the relationship between Christianity and tolerance, Aquinas argued that tolerance was a strategy or make shift tool for affecting a desired result in the short or long term, and should not be equate with virtue and grace. Expanding on this view, Yovel (1998) commented on "tolerance as grace and as right," and argued that in the past, tolerance had a patronizing character seen not as a right based on some universal principle, but essentially as an act of grace. For example, decisions made by emperors and kings about the suffering of groups were based on a unilateral proclamation or arbitrary acts of tyranny, not acts of beneficence and moral obligation found in modern society.

Numerous philosophers have examined the concept of tolerance. For John Locke (1947) and John Stuart Mills (1951), the concept of tolerance was a basic element of "civilized" society. Both argued that tolerance was a necessary social condition that would allow each individual to pursue his/her own good. It is therefore pertinent to state that by intruding on the values of particular groups or individuals without a thorough examination and understanding of their perspective creates a risk of doing a great disservice to the cause of diversity and tolerance.

For Mills and Locke, the idea of tolerance was also associated with individuality or uniqueness. Illustrating this idea, Locke asked, "Why am I beaten and ill-used by others? Because, perhaps, I wear not buskins; because my hair is not of the right cut; . . . because I avoid certain by-ways, which seem unto me to lead into the briars or precipice; . . . because I avoid to keep company with some travelers that are less grave, and others that are more sour than they ought to be?" Mills believed that tolerance was necessary to accommodate individuality, and that tolerance generated the problem of balancing this positive attribute with the tendency to carry individuality to an extreme in ways that challenge the social order. Tolerance, in other words, allows individuals to be unique, and should be valued. At the same time, tolerance may produce the conditions that lead to the undoing of society. Or, in the words of Glenn Tinder (1975) being tolerant allows "a chance of victory to thoughts you despise." To be tolerant, he said, "is to grant those whose beliefs you think endanger peace, or justice, or some other great common good, the right to try to win others over to their beliefs."

The crux of the problem was captured by Nunn, et al. (1978):

> Every society inevitably confronts the problem of how much individual freedom is possible and how much social control is needed. . . . If a human society is to persist very long, some balance of these needs is required . . . history has clearly shown that societies can vary widely from tightly controlled units to those that permit wide-ranging freedoms. . . . Some societies die from excessive social controls; others eventually fail from anarchy or from too few or ineffective means by which the collective concerns of its members can be met. . . . The more we learn about human groupings, the better able we are to specify both the conditions

that produce the differences and the circumstances under which more or less social enforcement of controls is indicated.

Furthering this discussion, Nunn, et al. (1978) wrote, "Diversity of attitudes and opinions freely expressed is vital to modern democratic societies. . . . Such societies must provide a supportive context for the development of these qualities."

Tolerance Across Cultures

Historically, America society/culture has been viewed as a breeding ground for diverse attitudes and opinion, or as a culture with a high level of tolerance. Yet, tolerance is not a unique American value. The preamble to the Constitution of the United Nations (UNESCO) adopted in 1945, states that

> peace, if it is not to fail, must be founded on the intellectual and moral solidarity of mankind . . .[and that] everyone has the right to freedom of thought, conscience and religion, of opinion and expression, and that education should promote understanding, tolerance and friendship among all nations, racial or religious groups". UNESCO declared that the meaning of tolerance includes "respect, acceptance and appreciation of the rich diversity of our world's cultures, our forms of expression and ways of being human. It is fostered by knowledge, openness, communication, and freedom of thought, conscience and belief. Tolerance is harmony in difference. It is not only a moral duty, it is also a political and legal requirement. Tolerance, the virtue that makes peace possible, contributes to the replacement of the culture of war by a culture of peace.

Tolerance: Social, Economic and Political Dimensions

Samuel Stouffer (1955) claimed that there were "great social, economic, and technological forces in the society that facilitated tolerance" associated with "the modernization process that increasingly presents different values, ideas, and styles of behavior to people." Clyde, et al. (1978) concur: "Not only are people exposed to this greater variety, the modern context structurally imposes an interdependence that makes heterogeneous relationships nearly unavoidable. . . . Diverse inter-group relations, though not intimate, broaden horizons and promote tolerance, and they are the basis of macro-social integration. . . ." This argument suggests that the establishment of accessible routes to social, political and economic opportunities is one mark of a tolerant society.

Modern Efforts to Define Tolerance

A number of scholars have attempted to define and clarify what is meant by the term tolerance. The philosopher, Johann Wolfgang Goethe (1953) argued that tolerance was a transitional attitude on the way to recognition, which may clarify the role of tolerance in society, but not the meaning of the term, especially as used in Western thought (Otto, Morgan and Walker 1995). Otto, Morgan and Walker argue that in the Western world, tolerance and diversity are often associated:

> Before dealing with questions relating to the issues of tolerance, a word on the category of 'difference' is necessary. It is important to recognize that the identification of difference is not a benign activity. Modern institution of government, originating in the social sciences of the west but now operating globally as the result of the 'civilizing mission' of colonialism, turn difference to the advantage of the status quo by fixing identities into precise categories

in the name of distributive justice and procedural fairness. The resulting statistical ordering and policing difference is a mechanism of social control central to 'good government', as understood in the modern European framework. In this way, difference becomes a disciplinary tool of the modern state which reinforces the dominance of European hegemony. These techniques have been promulgated at the global level by the UN charter which fosters a system of universal 'governmentality'. This makes it essential to interrogate the actual categories of difference, in addition to examining the hierarchies of power which these categories serve.

For Otto et al., difference is identified as a cause of conflict and human suffering, a negative liberty, or a tolerated "necessary evil." Continuing with this tradition of thought, tolerance can be used to harbor prejudices in order to contain the claims to equality made by subordinate groups. It further allows the majority to reinforce existing hierarchies of values while maintaining a 'veneer of neutrality' which purportedly values diverse categories and identities equally.

Lillig (2000) argues that today, intolerance to behavior can be traced to lasting changes in social structures including but not restricted to: the breaking apart of traditional family relationships; rapid transformations in lifestyles and religion; the increased complexity of economic and social contexts; internationalism; and the increased speed in the exchange of information. It is his position that these changes contribute to a growing confrontation between cultural, religious, and ethnic values. Lillig contends that increasing pluralism makes people feel insecure, disadvantaged, persecuted and dissatisfied, all of which may lead to intolerance. In this case, intolerance leads to the construction of identities that dissociate oneself from others as a reaction to frustration, excessive demands and stress. Lillig concluded that under these conditions it is very difficult to form a stable identity. This may result in the revaluation of one's self by devaluating others to compensate for lack of self-confidence. In this sense, intolerance results from reactions to social change that generate feelings of inadequacy and insecurity. Speaking to issues of direct relevance to this dissertation, Lillig argues that

> The question of tolerance is only raised in situations of conflict. The only time that the individual's own interpretation patterns, values and norms are questioned or violated is when these are confronted with deviant values or clashes of competing interests. The problem here is with the definition of deviant patterns and who is defining it and on what ground.

The author interprets his tolerance criteria to mean that individuals are to assess their own actions. Tinder (1975) distinguished between tolerance of expression and tolerance of action. For expression, he writes, One tries to enable another person to see things from one's own viewpoint and for action, one aims at altering an outward condition and is concerned only secondarily with affecting the minds of others--Delivering a speech, then, is expression and repairing an automobile engine is action.

In respect to respecting others convictions and values, some questions come to mind. Whom specifically should I respect? What particularly should I respect? And in what context? Suppose I am a member of the Black Panthers and facing a member of the KKK. I cannot say to him/her, I respect you as a person but not as a member of the KKK because it is his/her way of interpreting humanity. But I can say, I do not accept the KKK's stance on certain social issues; that is, I respect you but not the values of the KKK.

Aggression and Tolerance: Race, Religion and Difference

Historically, aggression in the name of tolerance has been a common phenomena in this country. The 1649 Act of Toleration was an assertive legislative effort by certain (catholic) religious group to protect themselves from persecution by other more powerful religious entities. Mark Cohen (1998), argues that in the search for solutions to persistent social problems, Americans have increasingly blamed the failures of minority individuals on "racial" inferiority instead of cultural differences, and suggests that social problems originate in the inability of mainstream America to accept "the social locations of difference." Differential tolerance can also give rise to some form of defensive interaction especially those buried in the old southern attitudes of racial superiority that responded to threats presented by expanded rights for African Americans (e.g., freedom, voting rights, desegregation, equal access to higher education).

Tolerance and Civility: What Ought to be Tolerated

Others, expanding on Locke and Mills, have dealt with the relationship between tolerance and civility, claiming that civility is impossible without toleration. This form of tolerance is seen in the way we treat each other, especially those with whom we disagree, and is measured by the "degree of courtesy" afford others with whom we disagree. For still others, the argument that some ideas and behavior are just plain wrong or "wicked" does not necessarily violate any meaningful definition of tolerance. According to Garlikov (1999):

> To say one ought to tolerate or accept certain behavior in others, even though one might not wish to behave that way oneself, or even though one might think it would be wrong for oneself to behave that way, is, I think, normally to ague that the

behavior under consideration is objectively wrong, but is merely a matter of taste, perspective, interpretation, preference, etc.....to tolerate a behavior is to permit it, to put up with it or allow or accept it even though one disapproves of it or thinks it is distasteful or wrong.......therefore it is not helpful to accuse someone of intolerance who thinks others are arguing for acceptance of a behavior s/he believes is wrong, and sufficiently bad to reject, even if that causes discord.

The point is that agreeing with what one deems wrong can be seen as being tolerant of immorality (or in this case delinquent behavior). There is little disagreement about the meaning of tolerance; what we usually disagree about is what behavior or idea ought to be tolerated. The disagreement is about what is right and what is wrong.

Societies, however, promote rules and policies that define intolerable behaviors, and meet those behaviors with sanctions. When a behavior crosses a group's or individual's tolerance limit, some may come forward to advocate that social rules be created to reduce or eliminate, and, at the very least punish that those who engage in the behavior in question if rules already exist.

Tolerance and Problem Solving

While many have examined the definition of tolerance and its role in society, others have discussed the role of tolerance in solving problems in interpersonal relationships. W. P. Vogt (1997) referred to tolerance as "putting up with something you do not like – often in order to get along better with others". For example, I like to listen to loud television broadcasts, especially sporting events. My wife hates loud television broadcasts. To compromise we moved into a house that has a basement. During the soccer, basketball and football seasons, the basement becomes my entertainment area. She can watch her HBO movies in peace upstairs. We both are able to tolerate each other that way. The point is that we had other options like separation, fights, or even divorce to use as alternative solutions to mere irritation. So we compromised our positions to the benefit of both of us and tolerate what we see as excess in the other. In this case, tolerance promotes compromise among people with different interests. Indeed, Vogt (1997) suggests that compromise is one of the important outcomes of tolerance. Viewed in this way, we can see that tolerance may also have broader effects outside of interpersonal relationships. For example, any social or political system built on compromise will also be built on tolerance, especially if such systems are based on non-violent or non-repressive ideologies. Such social system should promote harmony or greater social integration.

Tolerating Difference: Self-Restraint

Expanding on this idea, it can be seen that tolerance includes the ability to accommodate difference or diversity. Difference is often considered a precondition of tolerance; that is, if there were no differences among people, there would be nothing to tolerate. As an illustration, in their study of political tolerance, Sullivan, Piereson, and Marcus (1982; see also, Sullivan, Avery, Thalhammer, Wood and Bird, 1994) asked their subjects if they disliked a group, and only then asked them whether they would tolerate that group. The study showed that tolerance was only an option when one dislikes something and the distance between discriminatory and tolerant behavior is rather short. Sullivan et al., found that people tend not to be very tolerant of their "least liked group".

This discussion brings up a crucial point: tolerance generally involves inaction toward something that is deemed undesirable, or refraining from taking action. As discussed earlier in this chapter, inaction is crucial in determining whether a person is tolerant or intolerant. For example, defining delinquency as bad, but failing to take action when confronted with a delinquent behavior is defined as tolerating delinquency. Put another way we could say that "Tolerance is intentional self-restraint in the face of something one dislikes, objects to, finds threatening, or otherwise has a negative attitude toward—usually in order to maintain a social or political group or to promote harmony in a group whether small or large group as in a school or a nation...Tolerating a disruptive political dissent, rather than repressing it, may not be conducive to order and harmony in the short run, but it may well promote the stability of a democratic society in the long run" (Vogt, 1997).

Social Limits of Tolerance

All societies have tolerance limits. Rules are made in every society to restrict diversity and establish specific classification of actions that are, by definition, not tolerated. The most well known examples of intolerable actions is crime or delinquency. In the traditional view, crime is "behavior prohibited by law and punishable by a term of confinement, the imposition of fines, or other legal sanctions" (Davies, 2002). It is enough to say that all modern societies have established some type of laws defining crime, indicating, at least theoretically, that societies have a tolerance limit for certain behaviors. All societies have crime. Each society is creative in their definition of crime and in the sovereignty of punishment. Crime and punishment is a governmental action, therefore political tolerance is just as important as interpersonal tolerance. The existence of legal rules, however, does not mean that there is complete consensus within a society about its rules. Current examples include laws pertaining to drug use, the death penalty or abortion. For instance, in a survey assessing attitudes toward racial minorities, most white Americans (about two-thirds) disapproved of interracial marriages, but only about one- third thought they ought to be illegal (Davies, 1982; National Opinion

Research Center, 1986). In other words, the rights of others are a key component of tolerance. In this view, tolerance then may be defined as "support for the rights and liberties of others" (Corbett, 1982).

Dimensions of Tolerance

Vogt conceptualized and classified tolerance into two broad categories according to the traits and states of individuals who tolerates. The first is tolerance defined by its objects or what he called tolerates. In this category, Vogt developed three types of tolerance. They include political tolerance, moral tolerance and social tolerance. Political tolerance describes the tolerance of acts "in the public sphere, such as giving a speech, demonstrating, distributing leaflets, organizing meetings, etc…political tolerance in the united states often is referred to as civil liberties….important for winning and maintaining tolerance of other kinds." Moral tolerance is "tolerance of acts in the private sphere…most typically and controversially in recent decades are concerns regarding sexual conduct, such as living in sin, pornography, homosexuality, and abortion." The question here is which acts are private and matters over which the governments should have no control. The Wolfenden report submitted by a British parliamentary committee in 1957 is instructive in this matter, and established when private behavior should be considered legal or illegal acts. In *On Liberty*, Mill examined the gap between legal and illegal acts and argued that if an individual conduct is 'self-regarding', and has no influence on others, it should be tolerated, The Wolfenden report concurred. Finally, social tolerance is "tolerance of people's state of being; the characteristics people have at birth, such as skin color or language…" Such ascribed characteristics are sometimes the subject of intolerance, such as when America and South Africa where Blacks were prohibited from using the same water fountain or rest rooms as Whites. Race, it should be noted, is often the object of (in)tolerance.

The second category of tolerance is "tolerators;" or those doing the tolerating. This area of discussion is particularly important to this study. The idea to be emphasized is the cognitive or emotional state of the individual doing the tolerating. "What does it mean to say that an individual is tolerant or is engaged in tolerating?" It means that they accept the behavior. To accept the behavior, the tolerator must not act in a way that restrains the behavior of others.

Conclusion

This chapter has reviewed the history and various meanings associated with the concept tolerance. We have seen that the idea of tolerance developed from religious writings. It was also noted that the meaning of the concept of tolerance was broadened by latter social theorists. These theorists argued that tolerance is a necessary ingredient of a civilized society, as well as a cornerstone of democracy.

As a general definition, we can say that tolerance involves the act of respecting the beliefs of others. As an act respecting the beliefs of others, tolerance has two dimensions: an attitudinal and behavior dimension. The tolerant individual not only respects the beliefs of others, they acts in ways that do not transgress on the rights of others to hold or act on their beliefs and values. An individual who claims to tolerate a behavior must, therefore, not only tolerate the behavior as an idea, but also as a real action.

Tolerance, however, is not without limits. Individuals may, for example, tolerate a behavior that the society they live in does not. This creates a problem for the individual and for society. Those who tolerate actions that are not tolerated by the society they live and run the risk of being identified as deviants. The rulers of a society that maintains rules that are inconsistent with the beliefs of its citizens runs the risk of losing their legitimacy and run the risk of having their legitimacy as rulers challenged. Finally, a society that fails to socialize its citizens to accept rules that define the limits of tolerated behavior may experience other forms of deviance, such as crime, at rather elevated levels. If this is true, two conditions follow.

First, it can be hypothesized that those in a society who are more tolerant of crime may also be more likely to engaye in crime. Even if these individuals do not engage in crime themselves, their heightened tolerance may create an environment conducive to crime. That is, because crime is tolerated more so by some communities or by some kinds of people as compared to others, these groups or communities may experience higher rates of crime. This may, for instance, explain why rates of criminal offending are higher for men than for women, or in black communities compared to white communities.

Second, when a society encounters a situation where its broad definitions or tolerance of behavior (e.g., laws) are inconsistent with the level of tolerance expressed by its citizens for those behaviors, it faces one of two options. First, it can change its laws to be more consistent with the attitudes of its citizens. Second, it might be determined that what needs to be changed is the level of tolerance among the citizenry. Doing so requires the use of methods of socialization that have the potential to alter people's level of tolerance. In the modern era, the educational system has been called upon to replace traditional institutions such as family and religion in providing children with the forms of moral education (Durkheim, 1926) required to produced social conformity and tolerance. School age youths require exposure to value systems that help promote tolerance, and which define its limits.

Consistent with this view, data for this study were collected using questionnaires administered to students in public schools. This study examines tolerance in an open- minded and empirically manner sensitive to the meaning of tolerance as seen by or from the point of view of adolescents in this study. The differential tolerance of adolescent for juvenile delinquency will not be measured based on the simple claims that diversity and conflict are inevitable or that tolerance is an avenue used to quell diversity and conflict that may violate or approve others basic values or rights. Instead, we employ an attitude-behavior consistency model to test the hypothesis that there are differential adolescent or juvenile delinquency tolerance among different adolescent or juvenile race and gender groups.

In this study, tolerance will be, as in Faust (1970), defined as involving not only attitudes toward the views or expressions and actions of others which differ from one's own, but also attitudes toward the action to be taken when the limits of endurance are exceeded. Delinquency tolerance, then, is the acceptance of certain behavior defined by both an attitude of acceptance and a behavior of non-response. Delinquency tolerance can be understood, therefore, as having two primary dimensions: definitional and prevention (action). In this study, respondents are defined as tolerating delinquency if they define delinquency as wrong, but would fail to take action when faced with the same behavior. This definition of tolerance can be translated into a measure of tolerance, as illustrated in chapter five.

Before the data can be examined, however, it is necessary to review the work of Emile Durkhiem in *Moral Education*. It was here that Durkheim discussed the "proper" method for using schools as a form of secular socialization. This examination will be undertaken in the next article.

CHAPTER 2 REVIEW QUESTIONS

1. Identify and discuss the two major dimension of delinquency tolerance
2. What are the social limits of tolerance?
3. How can tolerance be effective in problem solving?

Theory of Delinquency Tolerance

Earlier, it was suggested that tolerance of delinquency may help explain variations in participation in delinquency. More specifically, it was posited that individuals who tolerate delinquency would be more likely to engage in delinquent acts than those who do not tolerate delinquency. This hypothesized relationship implies that tolerance of delinquency varies across individuals, and that it is this variation that must be explained in order to explain variation in delinquency participation. Since it is likely that tolerance is a learned social reaction, it is necessary to explain variations in tolerance with respect to exposure to and socialization into values that are more or less tolerant of delinquency. A number of different explanations that discuss the role of socialization may suit this purpose. Within criminology, several theoretical explanations of crime and delinquency that stem from the work of Emile Durkheim emphasize the connection between socialization/learning and participation in delinquency. Durkheim's work also makes an appropriate starting point for a discussion of tolerance, especially his work in the book, *Moral Education*, because of the association between learning social rules (moral education into societal norms and values) and tolerance for deviant behavior.

Theoretically, in this view, differences in delinquency tolerance result from differential socialization. This means that crime is not an attribute of a group, or an individual, but, generally speaking, results from differential socialization. It is likely that socialization differences can be found among intimate groups such as family, peers, classmates and/or communities. These differences are indeed an issue in the Durkheimian perspective, where variations in socialization can be explained with reference to the failure of society to provide a general and effective socialization experience. Adolescents who are not adequately socialized into the norms of the conventional society will be influenced by alternative socialization mechanisms that may reflect quality of life, economic security, anomie, developmental, parental, guardians or peer influences, or the effects of prevailing political and economic structures. In short, the failure of socialization mechanisms to consistently instill prevailing social norms and values to each individual in society, which was for Durkheim, one source of anomie, is the primary mechanism through which tolerance of crime and delinquency becomes problematic.

Durkhiem recognized and responded to this situation in his book, *Moral Education*, in which he discussed the theoretical process behind attachment to social groups, the development of morality in the child, and the essentials of human socialization connect delinquency tolerance to variations in socialization across groups.

It is a fundamentally held belief that the moral development of children is based on how they are socialized. One important variable is the rate of social change, which may stimulate and accelerate friction and conflict in society, creating a situation of anomie or normlessness. Under such conditions, adolescents grow up in a confusing milieu, become exposed to a variety of norms and values, and, because of ineffective socialization, do not possess the value system necessary to "choose the right path." Under such circumstances, it becomes more likely that adolescents rebel, or seek out alternative identities, and become more likely to be tolerant of delinquency.

Following Durkheim, understanding the socialization of adolescents into a state of "moral competence" may help us comprehend the developmental processes and how socialization institutions such as the family and schools influences delinquency tolerance.

Durkheim on Moral Education

Durkheim reasoned that socialization promotes stability in society and teaches roles associated with various social locations and places within communities or groups. Proper socialization promotes harmony and balance and prevents the tolerance of crime and delinquency.

A central theme of Durkheim's view on socialization concerns the source of social order and disorder. According to Durkheim, if an individual lacks any source of social restraint he/she will tend to satisfy his/her own appetites with little thought of the possible effect his/her actions will have on others. Instead of asking 'is this moral?' or 'does my family approve?' the individual is more likely to ask 'does this action satisfy or meet my needs?' The individual is left to find her/his own way in a world in which personal options for behavior have multiplied as norms have weakened. In this view, the desires and self-interests of human beings, which are the source of crime and disorder, can only be held in check by forces that originate outside of the individual. For Durkheim, this outside source was socialization and social structure: "if there is one fact that history has irrefutably demonstrated it is that the morality of each people is directly related to the social structure of the people practicing it… the connection is so intimate that, given the general character of the morality observed in a given society and barring abnormal and pathological cases, one can infer the nature of that society, the elements of its structure and the way it is organized" (Durkheim, 2002).

At the time Durkheim was undertaking his analysis of morality, he argued that it was religion that operated as the main force behind many forms of collective conscience, or that religion had dominated as a social force behind socialization. In theory, religious principles could act as a source of morality because they established the conditions that allowed the individual to transcend self and act for the social good by obeying the commands of god. In *Moral Education*, for example, Durkheim noted that

> No doubt God continues to play an important part in morality. It is He who assures respect for it and represses its violation. Offenses against Him…moral discipline was not instituted for His benefit, but for the benefit of men. He only intervenes to make it effective…but if we methodologically reject the notion of the sacred without systematically replacing it by another, the quasi-religious character of morality is without foundation since we are rejecting the traditional conception that provided that foundation without providing another (1961, 7).

Durkheim argued, however, that religion was a poor source of morality because it of its limited appeal and application. Not everyone in a society is subjected to the moral authority of religion, making religion a poor source for grounding moral beliefs. For example, the moral training offered by religion varied depending on the religion to which an individual adhered. In addition, not all individuals were exposed to religion. Religious rules and obligations that gave rise to morality thus varied too widely to serve as the basis of moral obligation in society. Durkheim sought an alternative socialization mechanism that all youth would be exposed to, which could instill a consistent morality. Durkheim argued that while all individuals were not subjected to the authority of religion, everyone in a society is subjected to the moral authority of the state. The state had also established an institution, the educational system, that could be employed to train or socialize youth into prevailing norms and values:

> If the eminent dignity attributed to moral rules has, up to the present time, only been expressed in the form of religious conceptions, it does not follow that it cannot be otherwise expressed; consequently, one must be careful that the dignity does not sink with the ideas conventionally associated with it...From the fact that nations, to explain it to themselves, have made of it a radiation and a reflection of divinity, it does not follow that it cannot be attached to another reality, to a purely empirical reality through which it is explained, and of which the idea of God is indeed perhaps only the symbolic expression...If, then, rationalizing education, we do not retain this character and make it clear to the child in a rational manner, we will only transmit to him a morality fallen from its natural dignity (1961, 10).

While transferring moral training to the school made sense, doing so was not without its problems. On this point, Durkheim noted:

> At the same time, we will risk drying up the source from which the schoolmaster himself drew a part of his authority and also a part of the warmth necessary to stir the heart and stimulate the mind...The schoolmaster, feeling that he was speaking in the name of a superior reality elevated himself, invested himself with an extra energy...If we do not succeed in preserving the sense of self and mission for him while providing, meanwhile, a different foundation for it—we risk having nothing more than a moral education without prestige and without life (p11).

The problem, in Durkheim's view, was devising a strategy that would transfer moral authority to the state:

> Here is a first body of eminently complex and positive problems that compel our attention when we undertake to secularize moral education...It is not enough to cut out; we must replace...We must discover those moral forces that men, down to the present time, have conceived of only under the form of religious allegories...We must disengage them from their symbols, present them in their rational nakedness, so to speak, and find a way to make a child feel their reality without recourse to any mythological intermediary...This is the first order of business: we want moral education to become rational and at the same time produce all the results to be expected from it...These questions are not the only ones we face here...Not only must we see to it that morality, as it becomes rationalized, loses not of its basic elements; but it must, through the very fact of secularization, become enriched with new elements...The first transformation of which I have just spoken bore only on the form of our moral ideas (p11).

An additional problem centered on how this transfer of moral authority was to be achieved. Durkheim is less clear on this point:

> The foundation itself cannot stand without profound modifications...The educator who would undertake to rationalize education without foreseeing the development of new sentiments, without preparing that development, and directing it, would fail in one aspect of this task...That is why he cannot confine himself to commenting upon the old morality of our

fathers...He must, in addition, help the younger generations to become conscious of the new ideal toward which they tend confusedly...To orient them in that direction it is not enough for him to conserve the past; he must prepare the future...Furthermore, it is on that condition alone that moral education fulfills its entire function...If we are satisfied with inculcating in children the body of mediocre moral ideas upon which humanity has been living for centuries, we could, to a certain extent, assure the private morality of individuals...(p13).

Even if this can be accomplished, Durkheim admits, the outcome is unclear:

But this is only the minimum condition of morality, and a nation cannot remain satisfied with it...For a great nation like ours to be truly in a state of moral health it is not enough for most of its member to be sufficiently removed from the grossest transgressions—murder, theft, fraud of all kinds...When the moral forces of a society remain unemployed, when they are not engaged in some work to accomplish, they deviate for their moral sense and are use up in a morbid and harmful manner...Just as work is the more necessary to man as he is more civilized, similarly, the more the intellectual and moral organization of societies becomes elevated and complex, the more it is necessary that they furnish new nourishment for their increased activity...A society like ours cannot, therefore, content itself with a complacent possession of moral results that have been handed down to it...It must go on to new conquest; it is necessary that the teacher prepare the children who are in his trust for those necessary advances...He must be on his guard against transmitting the moral gospel of our elders as a sort of closed book...On the contrary, he must excite in them a desire to add a few lines of their own, and give them the tools to satisfy the legitimate ambition...We can no longer use the traditional system which, as a matter of fact, endured only because of a miracle of equilibrium and the force of habit...(p13).

Considering the problems associated with religious moral training, and the difficulties associated with secular moral training, Durkheim concluded that: For a long time it [moral education] had been resting on an insecure foundation...It was no longer resting on beliefs strong enough to enable it to take care of its functions effectively...But to replace it usefully, it is not enough to cancel out the old system at the risk of jeopardizing what lies beneath...A complete recasting of our educational technique must now engage our efforts...We must resolve to face these difficulties (p14).

Most importantly, in *Moral Education*, Durkheim refers to adolescence as the critical stage of the formation of moral character and if we ignore laying the foundations of morality at this critical stage, it may be difficult to establish. It was, therefore, Durkheim's belief that moral education may, in other words, be the foundation for youth values that are less tolerant of delinquency. Durkheim (1961, 49) specifically emphasized the importance of moral education in the public schools when he wrote that "the public schools are and should be the flywheel of national education..." In contrast to the recent emphasis on family values as the locus of moral education in America, Durkheim noted "contrary to the all too popular notion that moral education falls chiefly within the jurisdiction of the family...the task of the school in the moral

development of the child can and should be of the greatest importance...for if it is the family that can distinctively and effectively
evoke and organize those homely sentiments basic to morality
and-even more generally-those germane to the simplest personal
relationships, it is not the agency so constituted as to train the
child in terms of the demands of society...almost by definition, as
it were, it is an inappropriate agency for such a task...therefore,
focusing our study on the school, we find ourselves precisely at
the point that should be regarded as the locus, par excellence, of
moral development for children of this age" (p. 52).

For Durkheim, the purpose of moral education is to nurture
socially approved forms of morality as a both virtue and a foundation on which adolescents can build a disciplined approach to life.
Since education is one of society's cultural goals and part of the
process of character formation, the cultural portion of moral education must be included as part of the system of public education.
The strategy is the development of prevention policies founded
upon moral strength that will elevate and empower adolescents to
challenge the tolerance of delinquent behavior.

Durkheim defines morality as a set of rules or norms that make
life in common possible. In this view, adolescents were to learn
social rules of morality in public schools and develop the spirit
of self-discipline that make it possible for them to conform to the
norms of the society at large. What is important is that adolescents
develop the sense of limits and constraints that is the basis of any
sound personality, the opposite of what hasd been previously described herein as tolerance. As you recall, tolerance was defined
as involving not only attitudes toward the views or expressions
and actions of others which differ from one's own, but also attitudes toward the action to be taken when the limits of endurance
are exceeded. Therefore, the main thing the schools transmit to
adolescents in the public schools is the positive value of group
norms that make it possible for groups to function adequately.
Adolescents must be socialized to be able to understand and

internalize group norms or social rules and conform to them. This is a difficult task in a society based on the premise of equality and equal treatment. When the idea of equal treatment is violated, certain segment, especially those who felt displaced, are forced to choose between conformity and various survival adaptations. These adaptations can manifest itself as tolerance for violation of social rules.

Recognizing the problems inherent in this approach, Durkheim added that the difficulties of establishing a secular moral order were exacerbated by the fact that "the child has his or her own nature, and in order to act intelligently on this nature, we must first of all seek to understand it" (p. 19). In other words, it is important to understand the moral development of the child when designing a system of moral education. On this point, Durkheim commented that:

> We know how readily and intensely a child becomes attached to objects of all kinds that fill his familiar environment...he suffers when deprived of them...it implies an aptitude in the child to develop solidarity with something other than himself...the child becomes attached not only to things but also to people...the child clearly experiences a need of joining his existence to that of others and suffers when the bond is broken...once accustomed to a certain way of feeling and acting, he departs from it with difficulty...he clings to it and, by extension, to the things conditioning it...he reproduces the ideas and sentiments that he thinks he reads in the faces of those around him or understand through the words he hears...everything that occurs in the part of external world within his purview echoes in his consciousness...his internal life is in no condition to resist the intrusion of strange elements...the

child imitates because his budding consciousness does not yet have a very strongly marked capacity for choice"(p. 49).

It was Durkheim's contention that "it is altogether evident that beyond the individual there is only a single psychic entity, one empirically observable moral being to which our wills can be linked: this is society…nothing but society can provide the objective for moral behavior…if society is to carry out the moral function which, from the standpoint of his particular interests the person cannot do, it must have its own character…there is one observation in particular that makes intelligible the unique character of society: this is the way in which a kind of collective personality sustains itself and persists through time, retaining its identity despite the endless changes produced in the mass of individual personalities" (p. 49).

Durkheim tell us that the "family, nation, and humanity represent different phases of our social and moral evolution, stages that prepare for, and build upon, one another…the family involves the person in an altogether different way, and answers to different moral needs, than does the nation…man is morally complete only when governed by the threefold force they exercise on him." The goal of a secular system of school-based moral education was to eclipse the limited ability of the family and religion to provide the social setting needed to narrow the limits of tolerance in society.

There was one large problem that remained, and which continues to frustrate the ability of secular moral training in schools to achieve its goal: variability in it application. The ability of individual schools to achieve the ideal of moral education varies widely. In large part, this reflects related issues such as the funding basis for schools. In contemporary society, school are less than perfect mechanisms for moral education because they reflect community resources, variations in community vales, and the effects of class and race structures that modify the general intended purpose of uniform moral education.

Beyond Durkheim

Durkheim's views have spawned a variety of theoretical approaches consistent with explanations of tolerance, crime and delinquency. A number of these explanations, such as control theory, are well known. Below, Durkheim's view is extended with reference to a number of explanations that owe a debt to Durkheim or which extend the discussion of moral education in the school system and which may be tied to the issue of tolerance of delinquency.

Walter C. Reckless in containment theory (1961) explains delinquency as interplay between two forms of control known as inner or internal (individual factors, characteristics or risks) and outer or external (environmental characteristics, factors or risks) containments. The theory shows how society produces a series of pulls and pushes toward delinquency. When faced with those barrages of risks, adolescents are forced to make choices about how to react to environmental stimuli. Socialization plays an important role in affecting the juveniles' choices, and the level of tolerance of delinquency they may acquire. Put another way, the conflict Reckless identifies may be an expression of processes that Durkheim specified as contributing to socialization processes that ultimately impact the juvenile's level of tolerance.

Building on a similar idea, Inkeles and Smith tell us, when adolescent change because of the influence of social institutions "they do so by incorporating the norms implicit in such organizations into their personality and by expressing those norms through their own attitudes, values, and behavior." Schools are very important socialization mechanisms for youth, and as Durkheim noted, can be employed as the locus of moral education. The school, however, is not the only important factor, and a number of "risk factors" can impact the development of values or behaviors.

Risk Factors

There are a wide variety of risk factors identified in criminological literature. Individual risk factors include early initiation of problem behavior, low expectations, for future success/education, anxiety or depression, aggressive behaviors, poor social skills, minority status and high levels of nonconformity and independence (Ellis and Sowers, 2001). Furthermore, family, school, peers, community and need factors are also regarded as negative risks that may affect the normal growth of children who are exposed to them. We are invariably continuously assaulted by environmental stimuli and we are bound to react to these stimuli and some adolescent response may be in the form of delinquency tolerance.

Finally, risk factors identify those characteristics, that when present in adolescent development will make it more likely that an individual will become tolerant of delinquency. For example, research indicates that low social economic status and poor parenting skills are associated with increased levels of delinquency. Risk factor may operate in a similar manner across racial group. The difference may also be the level of the risks present in racial communities. The level may determine adolescent tolerance of the risks and/or delinquency. Adolescent exposed to elevated levels of risks are very likely to be tolerant of delinquent behavior. African American single families are more likely to be headed by a female working mother who may be the only breadwinner for her children. The children have no role model but the TV animations and the local gangsters and drug dealer. The adolescent in such environment is exposed only to what is in the neighborhood and unsupervised. It is not surprising that such adolescent will be more likely to be tolerant of delinquency based on this exposure to risks factors present in the community. The position is particularly worse for those teenage mothers and fathers who have no parental skills or resources to help prevent delinquency tolerance. The poor family management skills, lack of clear behavioral expectations and supervision and other risks contribute to risk of delinquency tolerance.

Other Socialization Influences

It was stated in chapter two that attitude is generally defined in terms of beliefs or commitments and values are general attitudes defined sociologically, and norms are socially codified value about individual and/or group behavior. The variation in the conceptualization and definition is very considerable from group to group and individual to individual. In contemporary society like ours, the traditional source of socialization have gradually been replaced with what society thought was specifically designed to properly socialize the public to meet needs of a continually diversified society. The educational system has been called upon to do the job previously thought fit for the family, adults in the village and religion. It is hoped that education will produce social conformity and tolerance. Adolescents and school age youths require exposure to conventional value systems that will help promote intolerance of behaviors defined as unacceptable by society.

Race and gender have long been identified as risk factors. To account for this persistent finding, it was argued that there should be differential adolescent tolerance of delinquency among various adolescent race and gender groups. That is, there is variation in the tolerance of delinquency among the groups and among individuals. Tolerance of delinquency is related to socialization, the process of learning the values and norms of our society. Adolescents who are exposed to elevated criminogenic environment or crime rates and are exposed to elevated tolerance of delinquency are tolerant of delinquency. According to Durkheim, "society is the producer and repository of all the riches of civilization, without which man would fall to the level of animals. We must then be receptive to its influence, rather than turning back jealously upon ourselves to protect our autonomy... A person is not only a being who disciplines himself; he is also a system of ideas, of habits and tendencies, a consciousness that has a content; and one is all the more a person as this content is enriched… society, therefore, goes beyond the individual; it has its own nature distinct from that of the individual."

The educational system should be able to socialize adolescents from all racial groups equally. The fact that our educational system is not equally funded and some lack good counselors and teachers may well explain why black children are more likely than white children to develop tolerance of delinquency. Teachers are not trained to meet the need of the growing population of at-risk youth in African American communities. A lot of the schools black youth attend are also risk-laden, and are surrounded by the conditions that increase the risk of delinquency by raising tolerance of delinquent behavior. Children from these communities are more likely to be poor, hungry, angered, and lack the basis necessities needed to concentration on academic achievement. For them, survival and present oriented concerns become more important. The results of education lie in the distance future. Delinquency provides either an escape or a means for obtaining necessities or desired objects that education may not provide given forces such as racism which have contained the advancement of African Americans. Thus, Black youth may be more likely to tolerate delinquency because they understand how these acts may develop as reactions to conditions shared by other African American youth.

Following the work of Albert Cohen, many criminologists have hypothesized that these conditions may cause Black youth to reject conventional value systems as reflected in, for example, "Hip Hop" street culture. The response of schools as institution is to repress these expressions through dress codes. These are inadequate control mechanisms because they do not alter the cultural, social or economic conditions that give rise to alternative expressions. Dress codes do not, in other words, change tolerance of delinquency, and may in fact increase tensions that accelerate tolerance of delinquency among Black youth by alienating Black families and communities from the educational system. Black males socialized in such situations may gravitate to their peers, gangs and older more experienced deviants. Each of these social forces may expose Black youth to situation in which tolerant of delinquent and criminal behavior are the norm.

Stages of Development

The descriptions, discussions and explanations of adolescent behavior in literature are mostly presented in terms of developmental stages and are important in the understanding of delinquency tolerance. Generally speaking, adolescents become mature from stage to stage depending on how positively rich their specific socialization process and social environment was. "The assumption is that normal development proceeds through a variety of stages, generally beginning with a self-centered view of the world and progressing to a stage in which the individual makes choices in the best interests of both himself and the world…the failure to progress beyond certain stages of development may leave an individual in a situation where decisions are made that result in unacceptable behavior…the key for developmental theories, therefore, is to identify the stage at which an individual is operating and assist him/her in moving forward to a higher(progressive) developmental levels" (Lab, Williams, Holcomb, King and Buerger, 2004). But we also know that just the mere knowing or understanding of adolescent stages of development cannot by itself guarantee a successful socialization process. However, understanding adolescent development cognitively, physically, socially, emotionally and behaviorally is crucial to the explanation of delinquency tolerance. The Black adolescent's development, and especially when transitioning to adulthood, can be negatively influenced by the effects of racism, discrimination and oppression. Black youth are bombarded by stories of injustice. A report by the *John Hopkins*

Prevention Center indicates that black children and adolescents from poor communities experience a non clinical and non referral depressed mood which surfaces around age nine caused by low self esteem and morale, dissatisfaction with education, the loss of vocational aspirations and antagonistic stance showed by young Black adolescents. The experience of chronic poverty, dangerous and poor housing conditions, limited access to medical care, poor nutritional habits and instability of a adequate family life also contribute to their level of frustration. Exposure to stories of racism and exclusion, and witnessing this process first hand causes Black youth to develop attitudes that are more likely to elevate their tolerance of delinquency.

The theory of delinquency tolerance recognized that today's adolescents encounter far more social risks and face far more societal pressure to be successful in most aspect of life than adolescents in previous eras. Hamburg (1993) tells us that "today's adolescents face demands and expectations, as well as risks and temptations, that appear to be more numerous and complex than those adolescents faced a generation ago". Noam (1997) and Weissburg and Greenberg (1997) argued that "the majority of adolescents find the transition from childhood to adulthood a time of physical, cognitive, and social development that provides considerable challenge, opportunities, and growth...too many adolescents today are not provided with adequate opportunity and support to become competent adults...they are provided with less stable environment, high divorce rates, high adolescents pregnancies, increased geographical mobility and exposed to debilitating complex menu of lifestyle options". Thus, faced with such instability, delinquent identities may provide a sense of belonging for some adolescents. For example, research on gangs indicates that youth join gangs to belong to a close social unit and to feel loved and respected by somebody. This was the primary responsibility of the original family unit. Gangs are known to have their own norms which are usually in conflict with the norms of the so-called conventional society. Adolescent period of transition makes them very likely to join gangs to protect their feelings of inadequacy and confusion.

Adolescence is a critical stage in human development in which detailed information about society, social roles and expectations are continually transmitted, received and processed. Much of the information that adults or guardians transmit to youth may appear contradictory and involve double standards. The theory recognize that youths who lack strong self-concept or control are not equipped to properly process the conflicting information and are therefore more prone to tolerate delinquency. Shirley Feldman and Glenn Elliot (1990) describes society's conflicting and or ambivalent messages to adolescents as follows:

1. While many adults value the independence of youth, they also suggest that adolescents do not possess the level of maturity required to make autonomous, competent decisions about their lives.
2. Youth receive conflicting messages about their independence and status in society through inconsistently applied laws, or laws that specify various ages of maturity (e.g., for driving, drinking and voting).
3. Sexual messages delivered to adolescents are ambiguous as well. And involve learning to balance sexual exploration and pleasure with higher moral standards.
4. Age-linked alcohol and tobacco use regulations confuse or appear contradictory to youth who witness adults engaging in the use of these products.
5. Society promotes education and effort as values for success. Yet, youth observe others who succeed without much success, employing their natural talents in athletics.

In short, those in an inadequately and conventionally socialized group may become socially disoriented as a result of conflicting messages imposed on them by society. And because these adolescent cannot properly sort this conflicting information, they are forced to determine by themselves what they think is best way to adjust to the social environment. Some may choose to follow and adhere to the normative values of their group which may be inconsistent with the norms of the society at large. Youth in such circumstances may, therefore, form attitudes and values that are more tolerant of delinquency.

As youths move into middle or junior high schools at age 11 or 12, they begin to interact with diverse populations (including teachers and peers) with a plethora of social and cultural demographic backgrounds. In elementary school, the classroom is more likely to be experienced as a homogeneous social unit. According to Santrock (1998) "teachers and peers have a prominent influence on children during the elementary school years… the teacher symbolizes authority, which establishes the climate of the classroom, conditions of social interaction, and nature of group functioning and the peer group also becomes a learning community in which social roles and standards related to work and achievements are formed". High school adolescents are usually more aware of the school as a social system and may be motivated to conform and adapt to the system or challenge it (Minuchin and Shapiro, 1983). Hawkins and Berndt (1985) indicated that the transition to middle or junior high school from elementary school is

> a normative experience for virtually all children… the transition can be stressful because it occurs simultaneously with many other changes in these adolescents, their family and in school…these changes include puberty and related concerns about body image; the emergence of at least some aspects of operational thought, including accompanying changes in social cognition; increased responsibility and independence in association with decreased dependence on parents; change from

a small, contained classroom structure to a larger, more impersonal school structure; change from one teacher to many teachers and a small, homogeneous set of peers to a large heterogeneous set of peers; and increased focus on achievement and performance, and their assessment. Studies of late transition indicates that adjustment dropped during the post-transition—for example, seventh graders self-esteem was lower than that of the sixth graders.

Eccles, Lord, and Buchanan (1996), in their study of factors that mediate school transition during early adolescence, found that when parents were attuned to their young adolescents' developmental needs and supported their autonomy in decision making situations, the adolescents showed better adjustment and higher self-esteem across the transition from elementary school to middle or junior high. It is very difficult nowadays for certain adults to entertain stress and frustration. By anology why should adolescents be the exception? The complex social, biological cognitive and cultural development of adolescents with the accompanying stress and frustration is the type of risk factor consistent with delinquency tolerance. This situation is especially prevalent among black adolescent group who are more likely to grow up in environment full of social risks. Adolescent development can be a very useful arena for understanding delinquency tolerance.

Piaget (1954), for example, argued that our transition through life goes through four stages in understanding the world. Each of the stages are interwoven and consists of particular ways of thinking. Piaget reminded us that it is the different way of understanding the world that makes one stage more advanced and distinct than another. Piaget first stage of cognitive development is the sensorimotor (birth to 2 years) where the infant is believed to construct an understanding of the world by coordinating sensory experience with physical actions. The preoperational stage (2 to 7 years) is where the child begins to represent the world with words and images. The concrete operational stage (7 to 11) is where the child is able to reason logically about concrete events and classify them. The final cognitive stage is the formal operational (11 to 15 or 16). At this stage, the adolescent reasons in more abstract and logical ways to the extent that their thoughts are more idealistic. These stages of cognitive development espoused by Piaget deserve a closer examination. These four stages are important to understanding adolescent delinquency tolerance theory. In stage one for example, it will be necessary to be vigilant as the child begins to construct understanding of the environment. If for example the child continue to cry after it is determined that enough food has been consumed, it may be wise not to continue the feeding. This is a way of training the child to be aware of the implications of the action. This training must be consistent throughout the stages and should include every form of action that the guardians deem inconsistent with "normal" behavior. It is necessary that this process or training be progressively stern and consistent.

Kohlberg (1976) argued that full moral development is achieved by progressing through a developmental series of cognitive changes of pre-conventional, conventional and post-conventional individually divided into early and late sub-stages. Kohlberg believe that stage one and two are dominated by an individualistic and egocentric orientation and the later stages may be dominated by a broader social perspective and behavior directed at gaining approval and more complete conscience development. Kohlberg viewed delinquent adolescents as having their morality held hostage in the first two stages. The non-delinquent adolescents are more likely to have reached stages three and four (Kohlberg, 1973). There is consensus among researchers that delinquents may be predictably characterized by pre-conventional moral thinking than non-delinquents. The quality of behavior associated with pre-conventional stage is, perhaps, characteristic of the tolerance levels expressed by the adolescent groups in this study. Arbuthnot, Gordon, and Jurkovic (1987) review of several studies testing Kohlberg's theory, found delinquents perform at a lower cognitive level than non-delinquents. Future research, therefore, should examine whether tolerance levels is related to variation in their stage of moral development as well.

The Black adolescent group, for example, is confronted with several complex social, psychological and biological issues. The complex issues we believe will account for the delinquency tolerance variability between Black and white adolescents. These issues include but are not restricted to the impact of puberty, the move towards independence, peer group pressure, masturbation, menstruation, the new body and self image, the development of boy-girl relationships and impulsivity and group norms or socialization.

The period or developmental stage in which an adolescent is exposed to risks is important to the study of adolescent delinquency tolerance. Research indicates that the risk of violence for example peaks during the second decade of life. Adolescents who are exposed to violence in childhood escalate their violence in adolescence and violence drops off as they enter adulthood. This also explains delinquency tolerance at this stage. Adolescents who have been exposed to tolerance of delinquency and criminal behavior at an earlier stage of life are more likely to be tolerant of delinquency. It is important to state in conclusion that the adolescent developmental changes prepare them to experiment with new behaviors. These new behavior may include delinquency tolerance that may be expressed through risk-taking behavior including cigarette smoking, alcohol consumption, drug use, sexual intercourse and violent behavior.

Self-Image, Self-Esteem and Identity

How individuals adapt to our social environment may be determined by evaluations of the self -- positively or negatively.

Self-evaluation is based on our culture, values or socialization and this is useful to understanding delinquency tolerance. Culture is the core of the socialization process. The American society for example encourages individualism and children are just becoming more smart and taking advantage of the knowledge about freedom, competition, and the loopholes in the norms and laws of the society. Adolescents are socialized to expect these things, for example,-freedom, to have their needs and wants met by those around them, to fight for what they want to get and to be materialistic. This should tell us that adolescents share certain similar characteristics with others in our society. But they also have personality differences. Adolescent are different demographically and otherwise. Delinquency tolerance theory stresses the importance of race and gender difference for example, amongst adolescents. This difference may contribute to the significant variation in delinquency tolerance. Let us take Black adolescents for our specific example.

Some families are known to train their children to deal with the outside world including who to trust and who not to trust. Black families do what sociologists refer to as "race socialization"; the idea that give their children the skills to deal with daily racism in a society that predominantly do look like them. Jews and Moslems/ Muslims may socialize their children to deal with religious discrimination, and female children must be socialized in our society on how to avoid and deal with male chauvinists. Durkheim tells us that the school has, "above all, the function of linking the child to society...as for the family, it itself suffices to arouse and sustain in the hearts of its members those sentiments necessary for its existence...the school is the only moral agent through which the child is able systematically to learn to know and love his country...it is precisely this fact that lends pre-eminent significance to the part played by the school today in the shaping of national morality". To do so, and to instill more consistent values that lower tolerance of delinquency, schools must pay greater attention to religious, cultural, gender and racial training students receive either before enrolling in educational institutions, or while enrolled. For schools to be effective at the task of moral education, school officials must come up with plans that can reconcile these differences in socialization.

A larger issue may be presented by Erikson (1968) who held that the main theme of life is the quest for identity. It is his position that throughout life we ask, "who am I" and form a different answer at each stage of life. Erikson tells us that self-concept is a dynamic process of testing, selecting, and integrating thoughts and feelings about self and at each of the individual's sense of identity is reconfirmed on a new level. At this point, identity is transformed from one stage to the next, and early forms influence later forms. Erikson argued that adolescents in the midst of identity crises may seek temporary solution in over identifying with some popular hero, popular social phenomena or some social group to the extent of identity loss and that the crises is resolved through commitment. Furthermore, the general theory of crime and delinquency focuses on control through social bonds and that individuals who have low self-concept or control tend to get involved in criminal transactions and in this case are more tolerant of delinquent behavior and that it is a result of inadequate child rearing practices. Adolescent who lack positive commitment and or social bond to a conventional group are more tolerant of delinquent behavior.

Using the notions self-control and self-concept, it could be argued that the youth who join some groups are searching for their identities. The groups they join may affect their tolerance of delinquency as part of this process of identity discovery. That is, in searching for their identities, members of these groups are more willing to explore and accept delinquent identities than youth who do not join similar groups. This idea has, of course, long been offered as a cause of delinquency.

Self-esteem is another important component of self-concept in the construction of delinquency tolerance theory. Burchard (1996) in his study of early adolescence concluded that an initial drop in self-esteem may be likely due to change in school, body, etc. This stage is referred to as the period of the baritone for boys and other physical development for boys and girls. Furthermore, youths at the early development experience a weak sense of individual identity and need for peer validation. It is our position that tolerance of delinquency is possible activity for adolescent at this juncture. This is sometimes referred to as youth social revolution. This is when supervision is critical. Adolescents may begin to develop tolerance for a plethora of social events such as delinquency and social habits; make-up for example for girls and smoking and interest in sexual activities for boys. Burchard also found that friendships become sources of self worth and self-esteem, and important in the search for identity. Again, Burchard's explanation helps explain the difference seen in this study across gender groups with respect to tolerance of delinquency.

The main challenge of adolescence is change. They are faced with the great task of establishing self-concept, identity and esteem in the midst of these changes. The process of developing a sense of identity, esteem and concept may involve experimentation with differing appearance and behavior in interaction with family, peers and others. Those who develop esteems, concept and identity of outsiders and inconsistent and in opposition to family, school, community and peers are more likely to be tolerant of delinquency. Adolescents with low self-esteem for example are unable to manage their emotions, develop uncooperative spirit and are more likely to be violent and tolerant of delinquency. In order to improve self-esteem, concept and identity, adolescent should be provided with specific skills such as recognizing and managing their emotions, developing empathy, learning to resolve conflict rationally and learn to be part of a team.

Criminological Perspectives

Delinquency tolerance theory is conceived within the theoretical framework of normative deviance theory. According to Steinhart (1989), Stalans and Henry, (1994) and several other authors specializing in the study of deviance, it would be impossible to discuss deviance without reference to norms or expectations since normative expectations are the base-line against which deviance must be measured. The normative-deviance approach takes the view that deviance is always defined normatively. It is important to note that the normative order defines and creates the limits of acceptable and unacceptable conduct. In terms of this dissertation, the normative order helps to define the limits of an individual's tolerance for deviance, delinquency and crime. This observation raises several related issues.

First, because crime is an outcome of a political process where conflicting interests sometimes meet, at times law will represent the interests or normative expectations of some, but not all members of a society. Thus, when groups with less tolerance have more power and are in a better position to shape the law, other groups, which are more tolerant of deviance, may be placed in circumstances that enhance the probability that they will violate the law. In other words, while tolerance affects how crime is perceived and defined, power affects the ability of a group to translate their tolerance level into law. These ideas are consistent with the normative approach of Durkheim, the labeling approach, and critical/conflict criminological positions.

The critical or conflict perspective is considered a radical/Marxist derivative and its view of adolescent delinquency tolerance focuses on the social and political conditions that encourages delinquency tolerance. This view argues that to remove the elements that drive tolerance of delinquency, society must concentrate on changes necessary to dismiss injustice. Conflict theory is grounded in the belief that the American society is demographically characterized by social and physical segregations, polarized by class conflict and a lack of justice. C. M. Sinclair (1990) argued that "law is recognized as a social product and a social force... society is organized through exercise of power by a small but elite ruling class...society is held together by force and constraint... delinquent acts are so defined only because it is in the interest of the ruling class to define them as such". Those who's behavior are incompatible with those of the ruling class are therefore labeled delinquents. That is, the ruling class determines the level of delinquency tolerance based on their normative values. Behavior that is consistent with delinquency tolerance is regarded as a violation of norms and then labeled by a group of observers.

In a similar statement, labeling theorist, Howard Becker (1973) argued that "social groups create deviance by making the rules whose infraction constitute deviance and by applying those rules to particular people and labeling them as outsiders...from this point of view deviance is not a quality of the act the person commits, but rather a consequence of the application by others of rules or sanctions to an offender...the deviant is one to whom that label has been successfully applied; deviant behavior is behavior that people so label". In this view, adolescents delinquency tolerance may be better understood through a relativistic point of view.

Another issue lies in the fact that people are different and adolescents who are members of different race and gender group may be exposed to values that conflict with those of the dominant culture. This may make some (especially those who's behaviors are inconsistent with those of the dominant group) segment of adolescent population more susceptible to violating laws reflecting a lower tolerance of delinquency.

According to Durkheim (1897) "there cannot be a society in which the individuals do not differ more or less from the collective type". Durkheim also argued that "crime is normal" in the sense that a collectivity without criminal transactions would be deeply over-policed or controlled. Such societies would have relatively few crimes, but would never be devoid of crime. In contrast to such societies stand those that generate anomie. Alex Thio (2001) argued that by anomie, Durkheim referred "to an absence of social norms, which implies the failure of a society to control its members' behavior through laws, customs, and other norms".

Durkheim (1897) also argued "society cannot be formed without our being required to make perpetual and costly sacrifices." These forfeiture of valued individuality "embodied in the demands of the collective conscience, are the price of membership in society, and fulfilling the demands gives the individual members a sense of collective identity, which is an important source of social solidarity...but, more important, these demands are constructed so that it is inevitable that a certain number of people will not fulfill them" (Vold, Bernard, and Snipes, 2002). From a theoretical vantage point, this argument implies that groups that feel unattached to society because of racial or ethnic biases, or economic and spatial marginalization, may not share in the values of the dominant culture. Consequently, these groups may tend to develop values that are more tolerant of crime and delinquency, or alternative lifestyles and means of earning a livelihood. It is plausible, then, that adolescents that tolerate delinquency may be those who fell the sting of anomie.

Above, tolerance of delinquency was discussed relative to definitional issues and values, and the ability to translate values into laws. The society has the authority to prevent delinquency tolerance. Durkheim tells us that "in molding us morally, society has inculcated in us those feelings that prescribe our conduct so imperatively; and that kick back with such force when we fail to abide by their injunctions...our moral conscience is its product and reflects it...when our conscience speaks, it is society speaking within us... only society is beyond the individual...it therefore from society that all authority emanates. For example, in respect to criminal or delinquency tolerance, Durkheim argued that "Thou shalt not kill, thou shall not steal - - these maxims, which for centuries have been transmitted from generation to generation, evidently do not have in themselves any magic virtue requiring us to respect them. However, it seems to us an authority that constrains us, fixes limits for us, blocks us when we would trespass, and to which we defer with a feeling of religious respect…because society is beyond us it constitutes the only possible goal of moral conduct…we cannot seek to achieve it without elevating ourselves in the same measure beyond ourselves-without surpassing our individual nature." In any case, Durkheim added, "moral theory that does not begin by observing morality as it is in order to understand its nature -- its essential elements, its functions-necessarily lacks all foundation". But, tolerance may also impact crime by altering the likelihood that someone will decide to engage in deviant behavior, or perceive a behavior as acceptable even though it has been defined as illegitimate by society. In other words, tolerance may help explain factors that motivate criminal behavior. Thus, the idea of tolerance may help extend the explanations of criminal behavior found in several existing theories of crime. Some examples are provided below.

In regards to control theory, the basic tenet is that all men are potential criminals. And when one speaks of social control, one is usually referring to governmental bodies such as the police, the courts, corrections and their subsidiary units. There are other types of social control as well. It is these "other types" of social control that are the primary concern of control theory. These "other forms of control" include organized bodies or agencies like churches, schools, or less organized social formations such as friends, peers, neighbors and significant others. One can differentiate deviance from crime, right from wrong, delinquency from non-delinquency in terms of activities that arouse stigmatization, indignation or similar reaction within one's environment. Unofficial and popular or official attitudes towards delinquency or negative definitions of its tolerance can be a powerful force for juveniles. Control theory tells us that youths who have positive attitudes will resist the temptation of the violation of law. Kaplan (1991) found that youths with poor self- concept are the ones most likely to violate the law and engage in delinquent behavior. So for control theory, people obey the law because behavior and passion are controlled by internal and external forces. These same forces may control attitudes towards delinquency tolerance, which in turn will diminish the motivation to engage in delinquency.

Hirshi's social control is widely used to explain delinquency especially school related delinquency relationship. For adolescent delinquency tolerance, social control suggests that the school and school related experiences serve as social bond that restrain adolescent from tolerating delinquent behavior. There is a problem especially for those at risk adolescents growing up in dysfunctional environment and whose values are inconsistent with those of the public system of education. They are at risk of disciplinary actions, low academic achievement, numerous behavior problems and tolerance of delinquency as a result of inadequate bond to society and stake to conformity. Black adolescents are especially at risk of this problem because of the difference between the mainstream cultural values and the cultural values of African Americans adolescents who also are race socialized in their communities.

Cultural deviance theory is a combination of the effects of social disorganization and strain. Members of some group create an independent sub-culture with their own rules and values. Subcultures are clearly social locations where tolerance of delinquency can emerge. Sub-cultural norms, by their very definition, are in opposition to or clash with those of conventional values. When this happens, according to Sellin (1938) culture conflict occurs. Members of juvenile racial groups may be more likely to be socialized within such groups. Their values may be in conflict with those of the conventional society. As a result, their attitude toward delinquency may also be different from those of other groups. Cultural deviance theory may, in other words, help us understand delinquency tolerance as it relates to a juvenile's racial or ethnic group affiliation. It will specifically help explain why some acts of delinquency may be seen as acceptable by insiders and unacceptable by outsiders, and how motivations to delinquency may develop as the result of attachment to subcultural groups.

There are other "traps" in the poor and disadvantaged communities. This is especially dramatized in Black communities, which contain many risks to which adolescents may be exposed. These traps are in the form of drug use, violence, sexual indoctrination, abuse and molestation, inadequate education and negative role model. These traps are factors that fosters tolerance of delinquency. In this case, tolerance of delinquency may be seen as resulting from the kinds of communities in which youth are raised. In other words, there is a social structural element to delinquency tolerance tied to community characteristics which, in turn, are connected to the kinds of communities people from different classes or races are likely to live. Thus, tolerance of delinquency, which exhibits itself in individuals, may be caused by community structures.

Conclusion

In this chapter, Durkheim's theory of moral education was reviewed. Durkheim laid out the basis for a secular moral education in the school system that he believed would lead to a universal form of socialization. In this way, socialization should diminish variations in values across individuals, provide a strong socialization experience, minimize attitudes tolerant of crime and delinquency, and thus suppress crime and delinquency to a minimum. The problem, however, is complex, and, as was reviewed above, numerous issues impinge on the ability of schools to act as "perfect" mechanisms for socialization. Thus, there will still be variation in moral education. In contemporary society, these variations are expected to exhibit a pattern that reflects factors that influence socialization, such as class, or race or gender.

In addition, in today's world, many alternative socialization tools are available for influencing adolescents. Many of the tools for example, cable television, can be useful if properly supervised and maybe censored mainly for adolescents. The school is important but cannot prevent delinquency tolerance by itself. The work carried out in the schools must be reinforced elsewhere for a full positive result. The pertinent message is to take adolescent delinquency tolerance seriously and the to be concerned with the fact that adolescents actively shapes the relevance of their surroundings. Adolescent interactions with their various environments and their decisions on whether the social cliques they formed as they morally develop are relevant to delinquency tolerance. This however, highlights the importance of delinquency tolerance theory.

This chapter has attempted to illustrate that many theories that have been used to explain delinquency and crime can be amended to include the development of attitudes tolerant of delinquency. Theories of development, for example, lay out claims about socialization influences, and stages in life where these influences may have their greatest impact. It is also during these stages that attitudes conducive to tolerating delinquency may develop. Likewise, identity theories, which can be tied to stages of development, indicate that at a certain point in life when youth are trying to establish a unique identity, they are likely to join groups that have predefined identities. Some of these groups may foster delinquency tolerance. Membership in these groups, or the availability of these groups may have gender or race dimensions that would help explain the differential distribution of tolerance of delinquency across gender and race groups. Sociological theories, such as Merton's theory of anomie, discuss crime as a consequence of a disjunction between goals and means. These disjunctions, which may occur at different stages in life such as the transition from childhood to adolescence, or adolescence to adulthood, are also periods where youth are searching for new identities, which may be facilitated by joining different groups. Thus, anomie may be the driving force behind circumstances that expose youth to different cultural values that either favor or reject delinquency and crime as legitimate responses to the conditions they experience. Finally, the idea of tolerance can also be fit into one of the most popular sociological theories of crime and delinquency, social control theory. Social control explains crime with respect to bonding patterns. Those who lack bonds to conventional social order are postulated to be those who are more likely to engage in crime and delinquency. They may do so because once unattached from social order, they develop attitudes tolerant of delinquency.

In sum, the theory of tolerance pursued here is not necessarily seen as a stand alone theoretical explanation, but as an adjunct explanation that can be attached to a wide variety of explanations criminologists currently employ. These connections while plausible, and in many cases, self evident, are not worth developing extensively at this point until the initial evidence offered in this dissertation is assessed. It is, however, necessary to provide a further review of relevant criminological literature pertaining to the causes of crime and delinquency. This review is found in the chapter that follows.

CHAPTER 3 REVIEW QUESTIONS

1. Explain Durkheim's contribution to understanding of delinquency tolerance
2. What theories of development contribute to understanding delinquency tolerance?
3. To what extent is socialization critical to delinquency tolerance?

Review of the Literature

The Essence of the Problem

It would be unusual to discover a school-aged child that had not had any direct experience with juvenile misconduct, either as the victim or as the perpetrator, or both. Numerous social scientists, from psychologists who study the formation of attitudes and values, to criminologists interested in the fear of crime, hypothesize that these kinds of direct experiences shape an individual's attitudes. Because personal experiences are vast, it may be nearly impossible to know with any degree of certainty whether and how experience with criminal or delinquent events affect a person's attitudes, or how those experiences change their attitudes. Answering this kind of question would require administering a questionnaire through a longitudinal panel study design. Even with such a design, it is unlikely that an adequate and reasonable (in terms of length) questionnaire could be constructed. Furthermore, the individuals in the study would have to be followed from the earliest points in their lives if researchers desired to pin-point factors that affect attitudes.

Despite the foregoing stipulation, it is still possible to ask juveniles about their tolerance limits (attitudes) towards juvenile delinquency and to study the relationship between tolerance and behavior without being able to directly use the research results to discuss the etiology of tolerance and delinquency. Previous research, however, has addressed the causes of delinquency. This chapter will review some of the relevant perspectives that may also be linked to tolerance.

Juvenile Delinquency

Earlier it was noted that diversity in culture and values tends to locate definitions of juvenile delinquency individually. For example, juvenile delinquency can be seen differently from society to society, group to group, from subgroup to subgroup, from person to person (e.g., juvenile to juvenile), and across gender and racial groups. These attitudes about delinquency – delinquency tolerance – may or may not reflect existing, formal or legal definitions of delinquency. Consider, for instance, Werthman's (1963) observation that the "lower-class Negro boy does not routinely accept the authority of teachers, as is the tendency of the middle-class White boy." As Faust (1970) stated even intelligent African-American youth are "handicapped by this attitude in their attempts to gain an education, and it is the cause of much classroom conflict and school-related delinquency." Werthman (1963) adds that "many Negro boys who really want an education remain away from school in order to avoid facing authoritarian teachers and that they are supported in their truancy by their parents and peers." In effect, even though truancy is illegal, Black youth may have a high level of tolerance for this activity, which, in part, explains why they are willing to rely upon truancy as a solution to problems they face in school. Black youth's tolerance of truancy is not a simple "cultural" problem, but may have historical roots in the development of American society and prohibitions against Black education.

It is also possible that values within ghetto communities may support (tolerate) and even encourage these kinds of behaviors. Faust (1970:5) tells us that "an understanding of the specific group's definition of tolerance limits would, then, be essential to a meaningful analysis of the nature, extent, and causes of juvenile delinquency in that community."

Some forms of delinquency are tolerated, while other forms are not. But, even behavior that is not tolerated may not be acted upon. This is why it is important to measure various dimensions of tolerance, including whether youths report known offenses to authorities or others. The obvious source of information about reporting is the records of official reports (UCR), self-report studies, and victimization surveys. To be sure, whether a juvenile reports a violation may depend not only on their tolerance limits alone, but also other factors such as the relationship between the victim and the perpetrator, fear of reprisal, gang membership of the perpetrator, lack of confidence in law enforcement personnel, whether the violation was between family members, etc. It is important to note here also that attitude toward reporting a violation of law may be race, or gender based. This is one of the hypotheses that will be examined.

In his article "The Crime Problem," Walter C. Reckless (1961) tell us that "it should be clear that the definition of juvenile delinquency is more dependent on reporting vicissitudes than on violational behavior itself." Or, as Faust (1970) noted, "Reporting dimension of delinquency tolerance is the people's attitudes about what should be reported". And juveniles, like other members of society, have opinions about what to do when they see a law being violated. In fact, it can be said that all juveniles can have opinions about delinquent behavior. It may be important as well to consider these opinions in the design, and implementation of juvenile correction, prevention, or intervention programs.

Theoretical Consideration

The conceptual ramification of tolerance is pregnant with meanings. Tolerance, as used here, is a measure of attitude-behavior consistency with respect to definitions and reactions to delinquent behaviors. Several related issues are relevant to this discussion.

Attitudes

Attitudes involve making social judgments or evaluations. Weiten (1994) tells us that social psychologists' interest in attitude is legendary and that social psychology was defined in its early days as the study of attitudes.

In defining attitudes, McGuire (1985) noted that attitudes are orientations that locate objects of thought on dimensions of judgment. "Objects of thought" may be composed of social issues, groups, institutions, people and their products, and the like; whereas "dimensions of judgment" are those different ways in which individuals might make favorable or unfavorable evaluations of the object of their thought (Weiten, 1994). Weiten (1994) asserts that attitudes are complex mixtures of cognitive, emotional, and behavioral components:

> Cognitive component of an attitude is made up of the beliefs that people hold about the object of an attitude; the affective component of an attitude consists of the emotional feelings stimulated by an attitude object; while the behavioral component of an attitude consists of predisposition to act in certain ways toward an attitude object.

McGuire (1985) argues that numerous studies have shown that attitudes are mediocre predictors of people's behavior and that social psychologists have found, for example, that a favorable attitude toward a candidate may not translate into a vote for the candidate. Weigel, Vernon, and Tognacci (1974) contend that attitude-behavior inconsistencies may be the reason that people often discuss the cognitive and affective components of their attitudes (beliefs and feelings) in a general way that is not likely to predict specific behavior.

DeFleur and Westie (1989) also distinguished between two conceptions of attitude: probability and conception. Probability specifies that an attitude is commensurate with "the probability of recurrence of behavior in a given direction. The 'latent variable' conception "posits attitude as an intervening variable operating between stimulus and response, and inferred from overt behavior" (Faust, 1970). In his discussion of the two conceptions, Faust (1970:10) asserted that:

> It is implied that observable organization of behavior (behavior with consistency and direction) is due to, or explained by, the action of some mediating latent variable (i.e., some hypothetical variable, functioning within the individual which gives both direction and consistency to his behavior.

Defleur and Westie (1989) expected correspondence in terms of consistency between one behavioral dimension and another (i.e., verbal behavior, overt nonverbal behavior, and emotional-autonomic behavior), rather than between general latent attitudes and behavior.

Consistent with this psychological view on attitudes, the survey employed in the present research asked respondents about their attitudes (tolerance) of delinquency, their delinquent behaviors, and whether they reported (took their attitudes into consideration) observed delinquent acts.

Race

Race is often used as a covariate of crime and delinquency. Race in this study is seen as a covariate of tolerance. So one important variable that may affect tolerance of delinquency, reporting of delinquent acts and participation in delinquency is race. The measurement and operational definition of race can be found in the methods section Because race is employed as a variable in this study, a brief analysis of this term is provided in the methods section of chapter five.

Research indicates association or variation delinquency and race or ethnicity and it reflects social, cultural and economic differences among groups demand a sociological explanation. Delinquency tolerance is expected to covary with race based on the literature available on the association between these variables. Evidence suggests that blacks for example, may live in an elevated criminogenic environment, and have higher crime rates than whites, even when similar demographic characteristics are compared. Tolerance of delinquency is more activated in the black community and adolescents are readily exposed to social risks and as such may be more tolerance of the behavior.

Gender

Two of the oldest and most widely accepted conclusions in criminology are first, that involvement in crime diminishes with age, and second, that males are more likely than females to offend at every age. Criminal behavior, delinquency, or deviant behavior has been described in literature as male behavior. It would be intelligible to investigate female criminality and the differences noted in comparison to male criminality in order to understand delinquency and gender differences. In order to examine delinquency tolerance in terms of sex, it is necessary to examine previous materials relating to gender and criminal involvement. The most accessible source of data may be the FBI arrest statistics, which are the readily available official data.

When official statistics have been examined, it has been argued that there is a cleavage between male and female delinquency; specifically, female delinquency has often been viewed as revolving around "sex" delinquency while male delinquency has been viewed as centering largely around property offenses. Studies using self-report methods have found female delinquents to be more diversified and to be somewhat more similar to male delinquents than official statistics would indicate. . . In the final analysis of his study, Hindelberg found that the mean frequency of male delinquency is significantly greater than that of female delinquency for all activities except hit-and-run accidents and non-marijuana drug activities. This finding is consistent with the stereotypic view of the relative incidence of male and female delinquent involvement (Weis et al., 1996)

The above depicts rates calculated for both males and females age 10 through 64 for the 1960-1975-1990 population at risk, female percentage of arrests, and the profiles of male and female offenders. According to Shelley (1995) this finding:

For both males and females, arrest rates increased in some categories, decreased in others, and did not change in still others. The overall pattern of change was similar for both sexes. . . . This suggests that the rates of both sexes are influenced by similar social and legal forces, independent of any condition unique to women; the similarities in male and female offending patterns outnumber the differences. The similarities between the male and female profiles and their arrest trends are considerable. The most important gender differences in arrest profiles involve the proportionately greater involvement of women in minor property crimes such as larceny and fraud, and the relatively greater involvement of males in crimes against persons and major property crimes. The relatively high involvement of females is minor property crimes, coupled with their low involvement in the more "masculine" or serious kinds of violent and property crime, is found in most comparisons of gender differences in crime and delinquency. . . . For a number of categories, the female percentage of arrests has held steady or declined slightly, including arrests for homicide, aggravated assault, public drunkenness, drugs, and a few of the sex-related crimes.

In his conclusion, Shelley (1995) wrote that:

Relative to males, female involvement in crime or delinquency, past and present, is greatest in prostitution and sex-related public order offenses like vagrancy, disorderly conduct, and--for juveniles--runaways; in popular forms of substance abuse, in petty thefts and hustles and volumes of arrests for larceny in particular have become so great in recent decades as to have an impact on total arrest rates.

In comparison to male offenders, Shelley maintains that

Females are far less likely to be involved in serious offenses and the monetary value of female thefts, property damage, drugs, and injuries is typically smaller than that for similar offenses committed by males. Females are less likely to be solo perpetrators or to be part of a small nonpermanent crime groups. . . . Perhaps the most significant gender difference is the overwhelming dominance of males in more organized and highly lucrative crimes, whether based in the wider world or the "upper world."

Studies that explore differences in male and female juveniles' perception or attitude about conformity, deviance, right or wrong behavior, and delinquency tolerance are not available in any reasonable number. The few that exist in literature are worthy of note in this study. It is, however, necessary and important to first examine briefly theories for explaining gender differences.

Smith and Paternoster (1987) note that theories developed to account for male criminality are equally adept at explaining female criminality; the question is whether they can also account for gender differences in crime. Several factors may influence males and females differentially with respect to criminality. These factors include gender norms which are attendant on different goals in life for gender differences both for conventional roles and criminal roles, female beauty and sexual virtue, and nurturing role obligations of women that demand more consistent conformity than do male gender roles. For example, women are regarded as caregivers. Schur (1984) argued that

> Marriage and parenthood as major life goals have traditionally been more crucial in the socialization of females than males, and there seems to be little evidence of substantial change despite an increasing career orientation among many women. Women are therefore rewarded for their ability to establish stable family relationships and nurturing responsibility which in some ways render them less free psychologically and otherwise to initiate the "immaturity, insensitivity, and irresponsibility that historically have characterized the male criminal in relational matters", 1984).

Female sexual and physical attractiveness dictate closer supervision by fathers, shape labels applied to female deviancy, shape sexual victimization, and constrain their mobility. Juvenile males are expected to "sow their wild oats," juvenile females are closely surveilled. Femininity is another example of gender norms that feed on the weakness of female roles. Females are expected to be sexual, yet trained for warmth, nurturance, and to be supportive, weak, gentle, act like a "lady," wife and attend to the needs of all others. There are not acceptable deviant roles for females comparable to the romanticized "rogue" males. Shelley (1995) tells us that "the cleavage between what is feminine and what is criminal is sharp, whereas the dividing line between what is masculine and what is criminal is often a thin one."

The next factor in literature that is used in explaining gender difference is moral development. Galligan (1982) suggests that "male and female differ significantly in their moral development and that female's moral choices are more likely to constrain them from criminal behavior or delinquency that could be injurious to others." Females are more concerned than males about the needs of others, separation from loved ones, and tendency not to hurt others. Messerschmidt (1986) maintains that "In contrast to females, males who are conditioned toward status-seeking, yet marginalized from the world of work, are more likely to develop a perception of the world as consisting of givers and takers, with superior status accorded to the takers." Furthermore, such a moral stance obviously increases the likelihood of aggressive criminal behavior by those who become "convinced that people are at each other's throats increasingly in a game of life that has no moral rules."

Another factor is social control practices. Early and contemporary research literature showed that parents and most social agencies accord more control over girls than boys (Thrasher, 1927; Simmons & Blyth, 1987; Morash, 1986). "Compared to females in their early teens, boys more often are allowed to go places without parental permission or supervision, go out after dark, and to be left at home alone" (Simmons & Blyth, 1987). This may be the start of masculine training set aside by society's behavior toward boys. As this training progresses, boys begin to be exposed to risk-taking ventures, and delinquency. In contrast, female attachment training makes them much closer to parents, teachers, friends, and reduces involvement in delinquent behavior. Because of their "gentle socialization" by conventional adults rather than delinquent peers, females also are unlikely to perceive delinquency as being "fun," "exciting," or "status enhancing." Giordano et al. (1986) wrote that "among males, peer groups are a much stronger source of delinquent influence, particularly in the case of male adolescents with weak social bonds or low stakes in conformity."

Another factor utilized to account for gender differences is physical strength and aggression. Research indicates that aggressiveness consistently covaries with masculine criminality, and this trait is stronger among males than among females for reasons that are not explained by culture alone (Fishbein, 1990; Raine, 1997; Katz & Chambliss, 1996; Wilson & Herrnstein, 1955, 1996; Katz & Abel, 1984; Mednick et al., 1984; Walters & White, 1989; Mednick & Volavka, 1980; Prentky, 1985; Bowker, 1978; Hales & Hales, 1982; Olweus, 1988). Physical prowess, muscle, strength, and speed are hypothesized to be necessary for participating in crimes that are male dominated such as burglary, robbery, cargo theft, and hijacking, and for personal protection especially against competition and threat.

Access to criminal opportunity is another factor helping to explain gender difference. There are not be as many criminal opportunities available to females as males. This fact and the gender norms that have characterized the role of females restrict their participation and crime opportunities. Daly (1989) and Steffensmeier (1989) note that males dominate organized (Heyl, 1979) and more lucrative kinds of criminal enterprise, but not corporate and upper world crimes.

Rankin's (1980) study of attitudes toward education and educational performance showed gender differences in the relationship of these variables to delinquency. Though Rankin expected a greater effect on male than female delinquent behavior by these variables, his judgment was mainly a result of preconceived notions of a stereotypical characterization of males as more directly affected by occupational achievement. However, Rankin concluded that although negative attitudes toward school and poor school performance were significant predictors of delinquency among both sexes, the relationship was stronger for girls than for boys. This should not be surprising if we understand the effect of gender norms as it relates to socialization of both sexes. But in comparison to males, "the background of delinquent females is even more likely to be characterized by psychological disturbances (for example, low self-esteem, mental illness), extreme social deprivation or hardships (for example, poverty, broken homes, abusive parents), and situational pressures (for example, threatened loss of valued relationships)" (Steffensmeier & Allen, 1996).

Shover et al. (1979) reported that "the criminogenic importance of the traditional masculine role, itself, proved to be much less important than the traditional feminine role as a predictor of the extent of involvement in both types of delinquency (property and aggressive offenses)." This study was designed to make a comparison between masculinity hypotheses and the "opportunity" and "attachment to others" theories with the use of self-report sample. Even with increased opportunity, there has been no increase in aggressive female criminality as compared to males. Morash's (1986) findings in are consistent with Shover et al. (1979). The Morash study, designed to explain friendship patterns, interviewed 588 youths in the Boston area who had had contact with the juvenile justice system. Girls felt more embarrassed in participating than boys in such contact, and concluded that since girls tend to be in a less delinquent group, and had a lower delinquency rate (Morash, 1986, p. 50).

Albanese (1985) wrote that "Equipped with an understanding of the true nature and extent of delinquency, we are still left without an understanding of why it occurs." This is probably an overwhelming reason why it is vitally necessary to indulge ourselves in research or studies of delinquency tolerance. With the knowledge of who tolerates deviance behavior, it is possible to understand why delinquency occurs. This will be possible because we are investigating not only the demographic characteristics of groups but also the extent of involvement of boys and girls or males and females, when their involvement is significant, underlying reasons for their tolerance, and the age factor. However, theories of deviance behavior attempt to clarify why some juveniles engage in deviant behavior.

Explanations of Crime and Delinquency

There are basically two schools of thought regarding human behavior. The classical school asserts that human behavior is a rational product of free-will. As rational beings, people choose behaviors in ways that maximize pleasure and minimize pain. In classical theory, people are naturally hedonistic, and law and social control are needed to restrain people from jeopardizing the freedom of others. Cesare Beccaria (18th century) and Jeremy Betham (19th century) are two of the best known authors of this school of thought.

In contrast to the classical position, the positive school asserts that human behavior is determined by internal and external influences including biological, psychological, and sociological factors. According to the positivists, all people are not equal as the classicists would want us to believe; there are fundamental differences between a criminal and a non-criminal. The difference may be based on hereditary and environmental factors, including psychological factors.

Psychological Explanations of Crime

The psychological approach focuses on variations in the human psyche or what is described as internalized controls such as Freud's psychoanalytic theory. Freud based his theory on the interaction of the components of individual personality. There are three components to the personality according to Freud. They include the Id, which is said to be the primitive instinctive drives that everyone is born with, such as aggression and sexual drive. The superego is the conscience, reflecting values developed through interaction with parents and significant others. The ego, according to Freud, mediates between the desires of the id and the values of the superego. The interactions of the components of personality affect human conduct and therefore explain delinquency in terms of a faulty ego or a faulty superego (i.e., and unable to control the id adequately may result in an unbalanced personality that affects human conduct). Researchers studying psychological theories to explain behavior in terms of a weak or defective ego believe that a person may be unable to manage the demands of the conscience while facing real life problems resulting in guilt and in failure to resist temptations. However, a defective superego is commonly associated with deviant behavior by these researchers.

Researchers have attempted to explain delinquency with the use of Freud's components of personality. Jenkins (1947), for example, identified three ways superego defects can generate deviance: (1) over-inhibition, marked by an excessively developed superego; (2) an inadequately developed superego that fails to repress impulses; and (3) a "misdirected" developed around deviant values.

Freudian and defense mechanism based theories have limitations common to all psychological theories. First, self-report studies indicate that delinquency is so common that it will be difficult to prove that internal personality imbalances are equally widespread. Second, do these personality characteristics disappear, since most delinquents do not become older criminals? Next, these theories propose a tautological argument. Finally, as Albanese (1985) notes, psychological theories are not well suited to explaining why some juveniles choose crime over other reactions to personal strains.

Sociological Explanations of Crime

Sociological explanations of delinquency arose from the inability of psychological and biological explanations to explain delinquency. Sociological explanations look to the environment to locate influences that may affect behavior. Shaw and McKay (1942, 1969) gave meaning and impetus to this theoretical orientation with their studies in the city of Chicago. They found that high concentrations of delinquency were more apparent in urban areas of transition. Delinquency persisted in these areas despite cultural turn-over. They proposed a cultural conflict idea for high delinquency areas linked to social disorganization and neighborhood decay that could produce an environment that allowed for the cultural transmission of deviant values.

Another popular sociological explanation is anomie theory. Merton (1938) expanded on Durkheim's (1897) discussion of anomie, which can be defined as a disintegration of conventional norms and lack of institutional means to attain cultural goals to propose the idea that crime and delinquency result when means to achieve culturally approved goals are blocked.

Sutherland (1939) developed the theory of differential association which states that delinquent behavior is learned in the same way a person learns anything. Sutherland maintains that definitions favoring crime or conformity are learned from intimate personal groups such as family, friends, or peers. According to Sutherland, it is not the mere associations with criminals or non-criminals, but with definitions favorable to crime, that generates criminality.

Extending Sutherland's theory, Glasser (1956) proposed the theory of differential identification, which refers to the process whereby a person pursues delinquent behavior to the extent that the individual identifies himself with real or imaginary persons from whose point of view the delinquent behavior is acceptable. Jeffrey and Jeffrey (1959) revised Sutherland's theory by adding social learning, and maintain that the learning of criminal behavior is conditioned by age, sex, social class, race, and residential area. Burgess and Akers (1968) amended this perspective to included operant conditioning, resulting in the theory of differential reinforcement.

Albert Cohen (1955) elaborated on strain explanations in his book *Delinquent Boys*, and argued that the frustrated desire to conform to the conventional order causes nonconformity. Cohen's theory placed emphasis on the goal of status attainment among youths. Young people of different classes, races, and ethnicity are competing with one another for status and approval. Lower-class boys are less equipped and have fewer opportunities to achieve middle-class goals. Frustrated juveniles, especially from the lower-class who are more likely to experience failure and frustration in goal attainment), seek to formulate solutions to this status deprivation in a middle-class culture, resulting in a reaction-formation that replaces middle-class values with more easily obtain subcultural values. The solution is to act collectively as a gang subculture, where status is gained according to the rules of the gang. This conformity to the subcultural values of the group leads to violations of the norms of society. Cohen's theory does not explain the widespread delinquency of middle-class juveniles who do not experience status-frustration (Kitsuse & Detrick, 1959). Using a similar argument, Cloward and Ohlin (1961) suggested that youth use illegitimate means to obtain accepted societal goals.Walter B. Miller (1958) proposed that youth who experience deprivations and blocked opportunities characteristic of slum areas have distinct cultural values that remain stable over time. He noted that,

Delinquency is a product consistent with the values and attitudes of lower class culture. The street corner gang provides the first real opportunity to learn essential aspects of the male role in the context of peers facing similar problems of sex-role identification. . . . Since lower class boys are often brought up in female-dominated households . . . peer group is the most stable and solid primary group the juvenile has ever belonged. (Miller, 1958:5-19).

Miller sees the influence of the peer group as the mechanism by which adolescents become delinquent and that delinquency does not necessarily arise from conflict with conventional society, but it may simply be an accepted behavior in a stable lower-class culture.

Howard Becker (1963) gave impetus to a theoretical orientation with his studies regarding "tagging," stigmatizing, or "labeling." Giving the credit to Edward Lemert (1951), who originally put forth this theoretical orientation, Becker (1963) stated that "labeling theory hold that when society acts negatively to a particular individual (through adjudication), by means of the 'label' (delinquent) . . . we actually encourage future delinquency." According to Lemert and Becker, the labeling process depends less on the behavior of the delinquent than it does on the way others view their acts. Labeling views of delinquency are characterized by the fact that total delinquency does not exist and definitions of deviance change over time from place to place. According to Becker, there are more similarities between a delinquent and a non-delinquent, but juvenile public negative identification changes their self-image negatively and actually encourages delinquent acts with frequent and prolonged contact with the juvenile justice system.

Another explanation of delinquency is control theories of deviance, which are in related to strain, anomie theories and cultural disorganization theories:

> Those factors which are implied in the control of delinquent behavior: direct control imposed from without by means of restriction and punishment; internalized control exercised from within through conscience; indirect control related to affectional identification with parents and other non-criminal persons; and availability of alternative ways to satisfy the same needs that motivate other types of behavior (Nye, 1958).

Reckless (1961) version of control theory, referred to as containment theory, emphasizes internalized and direct social controls. He proposed that individuals are controlled through outer and/or inner containment and the outer containment involves social constraints to abide by rules and norms of one's group, while the inner containment or self-control is made up of beliefs in the legitimacy and moral validity of the law. Reckless included in this theory internal pushes, similar to the id drives, and external pulls of the environment. Therefore, he implied when containment fails to control these forces, deviance is possible.

Hirschi's (1969) control theory specifies how the elements of individual and social bonding (attachment, commitment, involvement, belief) affect delinquency. For Hirschi, delinquent behavior is possible when there is inadequate attachment to social units. When the bond is weak or breaks, the constraint that society places on persons are weakened or broken leading to likely misconduct or delinquency. It is Hirschi's position that everyone is a potential delinquent and that social controls are needed to maintain order. In a self-report survey testing his theory, Hirschi found that strong attachments to parents, commitment to values, involvement in school, and respect for police and law reduced the likelihood of delinquency. According to Hirschi, control mechanisms are developed through socialization and learning process and people who do not develop a bond to conventional order because of incomplete socialization, feel no moral obligation to conform.

Sykes and Matza (1957) argued that law violations should not be regarded as complete breaks in the bond to society, but as episodic releases in the moral restraints which surround law violation. They proposed techniques of neutralization which Sykes and Matza view as rationalizations which enable people to break the moral bind of the law and to break the law without feeling the effects of guilt. The authors put forth five basic techniques of neutralization which include: denying responsibilities, denying injury, denying the victim, condemning the condemners, and appealing to higher loyalties. These techniques are common tactics utilized by defense attorneys in the adversarial court of law.

Biological Explanations of Crime

Numerous biological explanation of crime and deviance exist. Several important studies suggest that human behavior is affected by cognitive processes that may be interrupted by structural defect and chemical imbalance in the brain. The question addressed by biological explanations of human behavior is whether some people are predisposed toward antisocial behavior.

Katz and Chambliss (1996) wrote that "Researchers currently studying the genetic, biological, chemical, and hormonal characteristics of criminals believe that, to some degree, the question can be answered and the relationship between biological factors and crime discovered." But the answer to that question created a dilemma for researchers during the early scientific study of crime. Early biological explanations – phrenology (Gall), stigmata and degeneration (Lombroso), moral anomalies (Garafalo), mental inferiority (Goring), criminal stock (Hooten), mesomorphic physique and aggressive temperament (Sheldon, Glueck & Glueck; Contes & Gatti), heritability of feeblemindedness (Dugsdale; Goddard)) – proved to be untenable scientifically (Persons, Roberts and McCandless 1972; Goring, 1913), and were criticized as classicist and racist ideologies (Pretchesky, 1979).

However, contemporary studies of chromosomal abnormalities, glandular dysfunction, structural brain defects, chemical imbalances, and nutritional deficiencies were more valid empirically. Contemporary studies in biology and criminality indicate that biological factors alone are not likely to provide the answers, especially since self-report studies have shown that nearly all juveniles engage in some form of delinquent behavior. Lamar Empey (1982) agreed and noted that

> The most objective conclusion would be that no final conclusions can be drawn. Nonetheless, we do know that, while efforts must be made to sort out the complex ways in which biological and environmental factors interact to produce human behavior, the prevalence of delinquent conduct is so great that we should not anticipate that biological factors alone will prove to be of overriding importance in explaining it.

Heredity and Crime

The first area of the heredity factor to be examined is chromosomal abnormalities. Usually, men have forty-six chromosomes; two of which are sex chromosomes (X only), collectively known as the XY chromosome. In 1963, Sandberg noted that some men who have two Y chromosomes . Mednick & Volavka (1980) argued that these men disproportionately represented in maximum security hospitals. Furthermore, the XYY men, they indicated, had an image of a "supermale" with an overaggressiveness spurred on by the extra male chromosome (Mednick & Volavka, 1980). A number of studies contradicted these findings (e.g., Witkin, 1977).

Another area in the search for causes and explanation of delinquency and crime is family and twin studies which "seek to identify genetic influences on behavioral traits by evaluating similarities among family members" (Fishbein, 1990). The study of identical twins has been employed to assess the impact of heritability of traits and environmental influences.

Shelley (1995:) tells us that "monozygotic (identical) twins are a product of a single egg and sperm, and therefore are 100 percent genetically similar; dizygotic (fraternal twins) are the product of two eggs and two sperm, and have the same genetic similarity as any two siblings (approximately 50 percent)." Lange's (1929) study of prisoners with identical and fraternal twins found that 77% (10 of 13) of identical twins were criminals and only two of the seventeen fraternal twins were criminals. Lange concluded that the higher level of concordance for identical twins was due to heredity, not environment (see also, Christensen, 1977). Robbins (1966) observed that a father's criminal behavior was one of the best predictors of delinquent behavior in a child.

Other heredity studies used adoption as a variable that might disentangle hererdity and crime issues. Mednick et al. (1984) examined a 4,000 adoptees in Copenhagen and concluded that the criminality of the biological parents was more predictive than the criminality of the adoptive parents, but the effects were interactive . "In addition, they reported that chronically criminal biological parents (those with three or more convictions) were three times more likely to produce chronically criminal sons than were biological parents with no convictions" (Wilson & Herrnstein, 1985).

Hans Eysenck (1964) argues that particular aspects of personality have a biological base and that a strong causative relationship exists between particular personality types and behavior. The two personality types of most interest are extroversion and introversion and psychological tests allow subjects to be located on an introversion-extroversion scale. The differences in placement of the scale are determined, according to Eysenck, by the genetically affected central nervous system (CNS), which determines reactions to external stimulation.

> The autonomic nervous system is the part of the nervous system which controls many of the body's involuntary functions. It is especially active in a "fight or flight" situation by preparing the body for maximum efficiency by increasing the heart rate, increasing the respiratory rate, dilating the pupils, stimulating the sweat glands, and rerouting the blood from the stomach to the muscle (Vold & Bernard, 1986)

For children, the primary socializing agent, according to Eysenck and other researchers, is the anxiety reaction in anticipation of punishment. Some studies of autonomic nervous system functioning have been conducted by measuring peripheral functions that are monitored by the defector. These functions are measured by exodermal electrical properties called galvanic skin resistance (GSR) or skin conductance. The responses of individuals are recorded as waves that have a relatively slow rate of change and are readily amenable to hand scoring. Emotional individuals were found to have high skin conductance; unemotional individuals tend to have low skin conductance (Mednick & Volavka, 1980; Loeb and Mednick, 1977; Siddle et al., 1973; Mednick, 1979).

> On a general level, this theory reduces antisocial behavior to uncontrolled responses to insufficient conditioning; it deemphasizes the initial societal choices about which behaviors are to be extinguished by punishment, as well as the fact that those who do violate this conditioning could be making rational choice. (Taylor et al. 1973)

Other researchers assume that abnormal CNS may be responsible for abnormal behavior. EEG is concerned with the different aspects of electrical brain activities. The EEG is recorded under resting conditions from the scalp and different chemical substances have been used to activate the EEG and it is said to be useful in the study of episodic behavioral disorders (Mednick & Volavka, 1980). Shelley (1995) tells us, however, that "the majority of studies, predictably, have concentrated on institutionalized populations of violent offenders."

Some neuropsychological studies focus on the results of the lateralized neuropsychological impairments study dealing with the psychopathism put forth by L. T. Yeudall and Flor-Henry in 1972. In this view, lateralized brain dysfunction of the temporo-frontal cortical-limbic systems is related to the genesis of the functional psychoses and criminal psychopathy (Yeudall, 1977). Yeudall observed that the "dysfunction is more lateralized to the dominant hemisphere in schizophrenia and criminal psychopathy and, conversely, to the non-dominant hemisphere in the periodic-affective disorders" (1977). Evidence of lateralized brain dysfunction was based on clinical neuro-pathological interpretations of the abnormal test profiles for the two patient groups. The results indicated that 91% of the psychopaths showed significant neuropsychological impairments based on clinical interpretation of the test profiles, affecting: (1) ability to formulate plans and intentions; (2) ability to evaluate the consequences of one's actions; (3) impaired intellectual functioning involving abstract reasoning and concept formulation; (4) ability to sustain attention, concentration, or long-term goal motivated activities; (5) the effectiveness of language to regulate behavior in terms of foresight or future behavior.

Different biochemical differences have been found to exist between controls and individuals with, for example, psychopathy, violent behavior, antisocial personality, conduct disorder, and other criminal behaviors. These groups have been observed on the basis of levels of certain hormones, neurotransmitters, toxins, peptide toxins, and metabolic processes (Fishbein, 1990). There is, for example, evidence that high levels of the male sex hormone testosterone may influence aggressive behavior in males (Fishbein, 1990). Testosterone is the principal androgenic steroid hormone and evidence suggests that its plasma levels and production rate may be related to criminal aggressive behavior in human males (Mednick & Volavka, 1980; Herrnstein & Wilson, 1985). Kreur and Rose (1972) reported that the plasm testosterone levels were higher in those men who had committed violent offenses than in the other men. Rada, Laws, and Kellner (1976) arrived at similar results in their study of rapists and child molesters. The research concerning the relationship between hormones and crime, in particular the male hormone testosterone and aggressiveness, to date have produced no consistent findings (Olweug, et al., 1980; Ellis, 1986; Mednick & Volavka, 1980; Shah & Roth, 1974; Prentky, 1985; Wilson & Herrnstein, 1985; Buikhuisen & Mednick, 1988; Adrian Raine, 1993). "Although a correlation has been reported between testosterone levels and aggression in young men, no proof exists that aggression causes a rise in testosterone or that increased testosterone causes aggression, or both" (Hoyenga & Hoyenga, 1979).

Tolerance Factors and Crime

To date, delinquency tolerance factor has been given far too little attention by policy makers and those engaged with behavioral research, especially those who may be responsible for establishing, planning, implementing, and evaluating public policies in the area of juvenile delinquency.

Several perception studies may help clarify their distinctions. J. D. Krause (1990) did a study on the perceptual impact of four neighborhood drug programs titled "Taking the War on Drugs to the Streets." He examined the impact of drug programs in four large communities by interviewing residents living in the programs' area and those residents living in comparable areas without drug programs. The results indicate that the programs were most likely to affect residents' perceptions of fear of crime, social control, and social cohesion.

M'Ottr and Giuseppa Luscri (1995) conducted a study about attitudes toward juveniles and criminal offending. The findings in the study suggested that opinions on juvenile offending have a similar attitudinal basis to opinion on offending in general. Although controversy has frequently characterized the subject of society's response to youth crime, there is a lack of due process rights for juveniles, disparity in sentencing resulting from the informality and wide discretion of the courts and child welfare authorities, lenient financial penalties, lack of uniform implementation across the country, and insufficient attention to punishment and protection of society (Hylton, 1994).

The few surveys of public opinion concerning juvenile justice have tended to focus on such topics as support for the juvenile death penalty, moving juvenile cases to adult court, sentencing, and incarceration of juveniles. There are a few attempts examining the influence of demographic and attitudinal variables as mentioned earlier, but none examined juvenile delinquency tolerance as this study attempts to do.

In the study of delinquency, group distinctions have been generally drawn along lines of social-economic, ecological, and ethnic characteristics. Huizinga and Elliott (1987) reported that there is a large proportion of offenders (84%) who are never arrested and that not all crimes are reported, known to the police, or result in an arrest. As a result, there is a large amount of "hidden crime" not contained in arrest data. In their study, using data from the National Youth Survey, the prevalence rates by racial groups for measures of general delinquency, UCR index offenses, felony assault, and felony theft, the findings indicated that in comparison with other racial groups, a slightly larger proportion of blacks report involvement in those aforementioned categories of crime, except for felony thefts where whites exceeded other groups. According to the findings, few of the differences between racial groups are statistically significant. The authors emphasized that minorities appear to be at greater risk for being charged with more serious offenses than whites involved in comparable levels of delinquent behavior, a factor that may eventually result in higher incarceration rates among minorities. The authors concluded that:

> A summary of their findings would suggest that differences in incarceration rates among racial groups cannot be explained by differences in offense behavior among these groups. The assertion that differential incarceration rates stem directly from differences in delinquency involvement is not supported by these analyses. There is indication of differential arrest rates for serious crimes among the racial groups, but the investigation of the relationship of race to arrest and juvenile justice system processing is required if reasons underlying the differences in incarceration rates are to be more fully understood. (Huizinga & Elliott, 1996)

Considering that valid characteristic features of different sub-groups within the larger society may be identified to permit meaningful distinctions, race is taken as one of the primary independent variables of this study. Generally, the findings of race-oriented studies by both theorists and research investigators tend to establish that certain sub-group ways of living, thinking, or feeling, or in fact their value system, is more supportive of, or at least conducive to delinquent behavior, especially as it relates to many urban minorities or lower-income class conditions.

In an intensive study of life in a Chicago slum area, Suttles (1969) found that:

> Since Addams area residents share many suspicions and common feelings, the content of their

subculture is limited in the direction it takes. First, there is a great deal of concern about illegal activities, the "outfit," and criminals. Those involved in these activities are small in number, but the residents are anxious to make peace with them or, if possible, to avoid them. Because they inquire so thoroughly into this issue, the residents are uncommonly aware of each other's illegal activities. The result is a sort of social compact in which respectable residents and those not so respectable are both tolerant and protective of one another. The subcultural commonalities of the Addams area consist primarily of a selective search for private information rather than the invention of normative ideals. The residents express admiration for unrelenting respectability, complete frankness, and a general restraint from force. In the real world they live in, however, the residents are willing to settle for a friend of doubtful repute, guarded personal disclosures, and the threat of force to meet force.

The findings of these and other similar studies, furthermore, suggest the filthy moral and criminal atmosphere in which many of American children are bred. It also suggests that tolerance of juvenile delinquent behavior would be high among members of the lower socioeconomic class. Most social science surveys suggest that lower-social economic class citizens are mostly minorities (blacks, Hispanics, Native Americans, and the like) with a percentage of poor whites. However, much of the research involving juvenile delinquency has been restricted to analysis of delinquency rates. As indicated earlier, race is considered as an important factor, especially because of the high statistical rate of crime and delinquency for blacks in the United States. Here we would emphasize distinguishing characteristics related to cultural, social, economic, and other related demographic and biological factors. Eisner (1977) noted that: "No one has ever been able to show that any biologically defined race behaves any different from another if all other factors are equal." He further asserted that: "Of course, all other factors are never equal, but racial differences in behavior are so bound with cultural differences that one is completely justified in saying that they are entirely due to the culture." Noted that cultural differences exist among races does not remove barriers in terms of social mobility for certain races; this may suggest a substantial observable difference in characteristics associated with delinquency.

These conclusions, although not directly related to delinquency tolerance, served as a starting point of this entity under investigation,

> Since they suggest that differential attitudes and values between racial groups might well be as important to the understanding and explanation of variations in delinquency rates of socio-economic conditions and concentration of police activity (Faust, 1970).

The contributions of the many authors cited here are significant in the study of juvenile delinquency and helped in forming the theoretical bases of this present investigation. However, these contributions have not dealt directly with the conception of delinquency tolerance, as herein presented. The problem presented by this present study has not been researched extensively or substantially. The largest amount of data involving conceptually similar concerns can be found in F. L. Faust (1970).

However, labeling theory is related to the definitional dimension of tolerance within the theoretical framework of normative deviance theory and the emphasis has been upon the labeling decisions and practices of school, police, and juvenile court agencies. Lohman (1981), in his study of juvenile delinquency suggested that "the description of a child as delinquent is primarily a function of policy, court standards, and community sentiment." It is true that these agencies have received a lot of attention and, though much of the research has been directed toward assessing the impact of delinquents' own self-labeling, the significance of juvenile assessment of delinquency tolerance has remained largely "a matter of conjecture beyond the point that the officially recorded reporting patterns of victims and witnesses may be construed as representative indices of such assessment."

It is worthy to note that the public opinion survey conducted by Louis Harris and Associates (1978) involving the interviews of a selected national sample of 1,000 adults and 200 teenagers is rather exceptional. The overall focus of the survey was mainly the perceptions and attitudes of the American public toward crime, corrections, and the administration of justice. The results were reported in terms of general public attitude, and expectations, and differences between whites' and blacks' responses, and a final emphasis about attitudes toward the dimension of correction, prevention, and control.

As it relates to corrections, the findings that are important to this present study are the tendency of blacks and less well educated whites to favor punishment of offenders and protection of society through long-term sentences, rather than rehabilitation, while the more educated whites favor the latter approaches.

In terms of prevention, blacks tend to favor federal spending on education, schools, poverty programs, and aid to cities more frequently than whites. "By a margin of almost 2 to 1, whites cited parental laxity more frequently than blacks and the major factor in the development of criminal and delinquent behavior, while blacks cited environment, poverty, unemployment, and lack of education more frequently than whites" (Louis Harris and Associates, 1978).

Insofar as control is concerned, both whites and blacks favored the conviction that the law enforcement system does not discourage crime, although they tend to feel that law enforcement officials are doing a good job. Whites, by a 2 to 1 margin, were more critical than blacks of court leniency, while blacks, by the same margin, felt more strongly than whites that courts are too severe in some cases and lenient in others. In addition, far more whites than blacks felt that most arrests are "fair," supporting the observation of contemporary studies and also that blacks feel that there is a differential system of justice.

David Greenberg (1993) explains youth crime as a consequence of the unique "structural position of juveniles in American society". It is his position that as adolescents develop and mature into young adults and structural position changes, they are likely to desist from crime:

> youths are largely excluded from meaningful partici-
> pation in the labor market for most of their teenage
> years. This lack of work places them at risk of ex-
> periencing three sources of strain that predispose
> them to delinquency, including 'achieving status or
> being popular with other adolescents requires the
> ability to participate in peer-group activities that are
> largely centered around leisure and consumption...
> money is needed to purchase goods and services
> that facilitate integration with peers.

Much property crime, the most popular adolescent crime according to Greenberg, results from the "disjunction between the desire to participate in social activities with peers and the absence of legitimate sources of funds to finance this participation". Secondly, youths are ignored by the capitalist system because they have no need for their labor and therefore daily warehoused in the nations public schools to socialize them into good and obedient workers. The school environments restrain their autonomy, they become frustrated and feel somehow humiliated especially the poor and unpopular adolescents. The result is aggression and then violence toward the authority restraining and contributing to their lack of means to participate in peer-group activities. Finally, Greenberg indicates that males experience the added burden of masculine status anxiety "precipitated by their worry over their anticipated or actual inability to fulfill traditional sex role expectations concerning work and support of family". In order to maintain these goals and their masculinity, some youths may result to delinquency by acting tough and violent.

The suggestion that youths who have jobs are less likely to be delinquent has been contradicted in other research (Cullen et al., 1997; Williams et al. 1996; Wright and Cullen, 2000; Wright et al., 2001). Cullen et al., tells us that from critical criminological perspective, it should be anticipated that youths who have jobs participate more in crime. It is their position that youths work mainly to satisfy material needs and are usually employed as cheap minimum wage labor. The job environment interferes with their educational goals, it is stressful, lack adult supervision in some cases, and fosters interaction with older, more delinquent youths.

Power Structures, Crime and Tolerance

The motivation to delinquency can be located in the structural position of youths in society. The motivation and willingness to act can be explained from the perspective of control theory. As a status system, the schools contribute to delinquency tolerance because by definition, the educational system 'embody invidious distinctions' where standards of evaluation are supposedly shared to reflect personal merit, yet those adolescents from the poor and lower status and backgrounds suffer self-esteem assault. Those who deemed to be failing in this status system, mostly from the lower class or minority groups are labeled and disrespected. In depriving adolescents access to the means of production the America capitalism generates delinquency and crime in a manner that cut across age, race, and gender groups. The nation excludes adolescents from the means of production; especially children from deeply disadvantaged backgrounds whose income may well be the only family sustainability. Adolescents like adults respond to this exclusion based on their structural position by delinquency and/or violence. It is therefore expected that those who systematically excluded or denied access to the means of production may well be more tolerant of delinquent behavior. Structural position may be a good predictor of delinquency tolerance. However, this is a society of laws and those who violate the norms must be sanctioned. The members of society at large are agreed on this point. Acts like murder, robbery, theft. Vandalism etc. are prohibited. Those who tolerate such behavior for what ever reasons or motivations will be in violation of societal norms. Control theory therefore will be another good predictor of delinquency tolerance because those who subscribe to society's consensus that laws of the land be respected will be less likely to be tolerant of deviant adolescent behavior.

The critical perspective provides an alternative explanation. Summarizing this view, Alex Thio (2001), stated that "in traditional or simple society, people share the same cultural values and therefore can have harmonious relationships with one another... such value consensus and social harmony are absent in modern industrial societies, particularly in the united states....instead , there is a great deal of social and 100

cultural conflict....this social conflict has to do with the incompatible interests, needs, and desires of diverse groups as business companies versus labor unions, conservatives versus liberal political groups, whites versus blacks and so on." Furthermore, cultural conflict has to do with the discrepant norms and values that derive from definitions of right and wrong---that is what is right in one sub-culture is considered wrong in another. For example, an Arab who decides to murder his sister because she was raped will be charged with homicide in the United States where as his action is tolerated in Arab or Moslem culture. Both social and cultural conflict has been used to explain criminal or delinquent behavior among immigrants, African Americans, poor folks and oppressed groups.

Quinney (1974) argues that crime must be viewed in relation to law-making. It is his position that the interaction among the lawmaking by dominant class, law enforcement by criminal justice system for dominant class, popular ideology, and criminal acts by subordinate class help produce and maintain a certain high level of crime and delinquency. This societal situation therefore helps maintain and foster tolerance and intolerance of certain behavior. Vold (1958) and Turk (1969), applied the ideas of conflict theory to the concept of crime and law when they examined the process by which laws are passed in society and found that because the dominant and powerful groups are able to exercise that power and shape the very lawmaking process that determines who and what will be defined as deviant or criminal, they also will determine what acts are tolerated in society.

The theoretical reviews, related research, the findings and conclusions, when put together or separately considered, would tend to support the proposition that there are observable differences between racial and gender groups in attitudes related to the several dimensions of delinquency tolerance.

CHAPTER 4 REVIEW QUESTIONS

1. What theory has more validity in explaining tolerance of delinquency?
2. Is delinquency tolerance universal among adolescence?
3. Why is culture important in explaining delinquency tolerance?

CHAPTER 5

Design and Methodology

The purpose of this study is to examine juvenile's tolerance of acts of delinquency. As noted earlier, little previous research has been conducted on the issue of criminal or delinquent behavior tolerance. In fact, no previous research project has examined the issue of tolerance of delinquency by juveniles to any extent. For example, F. L. Faust (1970) examined *adult tolerance* of juvenile delinquency. In a later study, P. M. Sharp (1983) examined one dimension of delinquency tolerance by juveniles, though this study's questionnaire allowed for an incomplete assessment of the full extent and multiple dimensions of delinquency tolerance by juveniles. As a result, those seeking to perform a study focusing on tolerance of delinquency by juveniles are provided with little guidance in extant literature.

In a review of previous studies on delinquency, Barri Flowers (1990) lamented the lack of empirical studies addressing juveniles' views on crime and delinquency. While studies involving adults' attitudes toward a variety of crime and justice issues are found relatively frequently in the criminological literature, the juvenile subject's attitude toward crime and punishment remains absent. In such an intellectual environment, it remains difficult to understand whether juveniles and adults share views about crime and justice, whether these views affect participation in crime, and the extent to which juvenile and adult tolerance of crime correspond or diverge.

Based upon the discussion provided in earlier chapters, several hypotheses can be offered. First, differentials in tolerance of delinquency by juveniles may account for differential participation in delinquency. Thus, within any given group of juveniles, those with the greatest tolerance of delinquency are expected to have the highest rates of participation in delinquency. This hypothesis is not, however, directly testable with the data collected as part of this dissertation.

Second, juveniles who have a high tolerance for delinquency are also hypothesized to be less likely than juveniles with a low tolerance for delinquency to report acts of delinquency to criminal justice officials or other persons of authority. This hypothesis is also not testable with the data collected for this dissertation.

Finally, consistent with the correlates of delinquency discovered in earlier research, it is hypothesized that tolerance of delinquency may be associated with other correlates of delinquency. The sub-hypotheses are suggested: (S-1) male juveniles would have a greater tolerance of delinquency than female juveniles; and (S-2) black and Hispanic youth will have a greater tolerance of delinquency than white youth. Hypotheses related to race/ethnicity, gender and tolerance of delinquency are testable with the present data.

Because the factors that affect tolerance of delinquency vary across individuals, the sample employed to test hypotheses concerning the relationship between tolerance and personal characteristics can be drawn from any relevant larger population, and the results of this research should not be impacted by the composition of the study population (unless, of course, the study population is constructed in such a way as to exclude comparisons across potentially relevant characteristics, or the sample is biased). In other words, the survey employed to research juvenile's tolerance of delinquency has no known geographic limitations, and could be conducted in almost any city of the United States. The data for the present investigation was derived from a survey conducted in Tallahassee, Florida.

The survey used in the present study was adapted from Faust's mailed survey (1989) on adult tolerance of juvenile delinquency, and updated to meet the specific needs of this study with the help of the originator of the survey instrument, Professor Fredrick Faust. The survey was administered to students in select classes on the day the survey was administered in the Tallahassee school system between October and November of 1998. Further discussion of the sample can be found below.

The effect of tolerance on participation in and reporting of delinquent acts will be examined at the individual level, or the school level. In the case of larger geographic sample, higher levels of aggregation may prove to be another important dimension of statistical comparison. For the purposes of the present research, the focus will be on factors believed to affect individual level variations in tolerance.

Background: Leon County Schools

In this section, characteristics of the Leon County school system are examined. It is important to understand the characteristics of the Leon County school system because future research conducted in school systems with different characteristics may begin to reveal the potentially complex relationship between tolerance of delinquency participation in delinquency, and community and school characteristics.

General Educational Rules, State of Florida

Each county in Florida is regarded as a single school district and, at the time this research was undertaken, was also considered to be part of the state educational system. As a result, each school district must follow the rules and regulations of the State Board of Education.

A county superintendent of schools manages each school district. The county superintendent of schools is elected county-wise, and also serves as the secretary and executive officer of the school board.

The Leon county school system is divided into five districts, each of which is represented by one elected member who serves on the county board of education. Each district offers all levels of elementary and secondary education The county school board is the local policy making board and each of the five members is elected by the voters who live in the district from which he/she resides and runs.

In 1998, each of Leon county schools offered pre-kindergarten through grade twelve (12) courses to more than 31,000 students who attended over forty school centers. The Leon county school system offered a number of additional programs for exceptional, special, gifted, and homebound students, as well as adult, vocational and community educational programs, the school for applied individualized learning (SAIL), and teenage parent educational services, among others. .

According to the By-Laws of the Leon County school system, the mission of the Leon county schools is to create a quality, caring environment that prepares learners to become responsible, self-governing, independent and contributing citizens in a world of change by providing leadership and an organizational structure through the combined efforts and resources of the community. To help meet these objectives, the By-Laws also specify that schools must be safe for attendees. Students have rights and responsibilities that contribute to a safe school environment. First, county school policy 7.01 states that no "student has the right to interfere with the education of his fellow students. It is the responsibility of each student to respect the rights of all who are involved in the educational process." Second, in a further effort to maintain a safe school environment, county school policy 7.12 state that "a cooperative effort shall be maintained between the principal and his/her designee and law enforcement agencies. Within this policy, a child may be taken into custody by an authorized agent of the state if any law of the land is violated." A variety of strategies are in place to quell any student delinquency. Students are not permitted to belong to any gang or secret societies, especially because maintaining a safe and orderly environment is an important responsibility of all educators. In addition, in order to promote a safe school environmental, students who are found to have committed any felony or offenses requiring severe consequences expelled subsequently referred to law enforcement authority (Zero tolerance policy). These policies may also have an impact on the tolerance of delinquency expressed by students in the Tallahassee school system. This impact, however, is assumed to be evenly distributed among the population. Its effects would only be evident – if it existed at all – when multiple school systems were compared.

Sample Selection

There are 25 elementary, 8 middle and 5 high schools in the Leon County School system. Originally, the research plan called for a random sample of schools from Leon County. In planning this research, a meeting was held with the Superintendent of Leon County Schools. The purpose of the project was discussed, and appropriate methods of proceeding were discussed. While the Superintendent was pleased to participate in the project, he preferred voluntary participation rather than a scientifically derived system of random sampling. The Superintendent left it up to the principal of each individual school to decide whether or not his/ her school would participate. Meetings were held with each principal to discuss the proposed project. Based upon these meetings, principals decided whether or not to participate. Eleven of the 38 principals decided to participate representing four (4) elementary schools, four (4) middle schools, and three (3) high schools.

Sampling was further complicated by the decision principals made to allow teachers to decide whether or not their individual classes would participate. Because principals and teachers were given the option to participate, the sample of students was not random.

Meetings were held with teachers at each school to gain their participation in the project. Teachers who chose to participate were provided with consent forms to give to students. Students were required to have a signed parental consent form on the day the survey was administered, or the child was not allowed to participate in the survey. Surveys were anonymous. The only identification mechanism employed was that surveys were color coded to indicate the type of school in which they were administered.

No sensitive information was requested from participants. Students were asked to provide their opinions about whether they thought a behavior should be considered criminal, whether they would report a specific behavior to adults or legal authorities, and what kinds of responses they believed would help eliminate the specified behavior.

To ensure anonymity, student responses were coded into electronic format, and only the electronic data were made available for the present project. The original questionnaire data was collected by Professor Fredrick Faust of the Florida State University. Professor Faust received the approval of the Human Subject Review Board at the Florida State University to conduct the research. Professor Faust, who has since retired and whose whereabouts are currently unknown, retains control of the original data.

The percentage of the completed questionnaires returned was calculated. Completion rates were affected by respondent's age. Response rates were very low in the 5-8 year old group (N = 25), and much lower than expected in the 9-11 year old age group (N

= 80). It appears that the completion rates in these groups were affected by literacy rates and vocabulary development skills that were age-related. In fact, before the questionnaire was administered, this possibility was assessed using the Dale-Chall formula for predicting readability or the reading level of a document. The questionnaire received a score of 5.9 score, indicating that respondents would have to possess nearly a sixth grade reading level to successfully complete the questionnaire. In part, this score is a consequence of the "technical" words required to be used on this questionnaire, including the words "juvenile", "teenager", "institution", "delinquent" and "deviant." These words were deemed unavoidable, and could not be removed from the survey instrument to improve readability.

In an effort to ensure the integrity of the sampling procedure, a follow-up procedure was employed to enhance response rates. The follow-up survey procedure involved an effort on the part of teachers to ensure that students absent on the day of the original survey completed the survey upon their return to school.

To maintain similar circumstances across test-settings, the teachers who were administering the survey were given an orientation-training session before the survey was conducted. The orientation involved instructions about avoiding any discussions of the questionnaire with the respondents that might influence their responses.

Social and characteristics of respondents were used to verify the representativeness of the survey population in comparison to the universe of students in the Leon County School system. The percentage of the respondents that falls into each subgroup of the characteristic categories (i.e., sex, age, race, etc.) were calculated across schools by location (west, east, north, south), and the existence of significant differences were estimated using the Lawshe-Baker Nomograph. By locating a line between the two percentages (P_1 and P_2) on inverse scales, the omega value can be read on the nomograph and it can be immediately determined if the difference between the two is significant at the .05 level. Using this procedure, it was determined that the sample, though not random, was representative of the population of Leon County's schools.

Construction of the Questionnaire

The survey instrument was adapted from Faust (1970). The survey was modified to meet the need of this study. The Fauust questionnaire was used to survey adult attitudes toward delinquency. The main idea of the Faust survey materials was very much suitable for the present study. In the first three sections of the survey that deals with the definitional, reporting and correction dimension of delinquency tolerance, Faust had only nine questions for each dimension. This study survey improved the questions to fifteen questions for each dimension by adding more questions that we hope will reveal adolescent attitude toward and tolerance of delinquency. Questions relating to possession of a gun at school or home, marijuana use, destruction of property, etc. were added to aid in this effort. In the next section on prevention where we asked would the following things help cut the amount of delinquency?, we also added four more options for controlling and preventing delinquency tolerance. In all of the dimensions mentioned, we did not have to change some technical terms. Teachers were allowed to interpret certain terms to participants to allow juveniles to be able to understand and answer the questions. In section that demanded demographic facts about the participants, we changed man/woman to boys and girls The survey instrument began with a concise statement regarding the purpose of the study. It also included an appeal for assistance in completing the research project by completing the survey and instructions for completing and turning in the questionnaire.

The first section of the questionnaire was designed to elicit information about each respondent social characteristics (i.e., gender, race, age, grade level, school). The second section included one question that pertain to determining a youth's tolerance of nine different behavioral acts. The question in this section stated: "If you saw other children (juveniles) from your neighborhood doing the following things, would you feel that they were wrong or right (delinquent or non-delinquent)?" Nine different juvenile delinquent behaviors were listed, and the respondent was asked to indicate whether he or she believed that the behavior was "delinquent" or "wrong" or "non delinquent" or "acceptable."

The second tolerance related section addresses the social control dimension of tolerance, and asked: "If you saw other children (juveniles) from your neighborhood doing the following things, would you do nothing, report it to the teachers, parents, police, or other authority, or do something to protect yourself?" The same nine juvenile behavior items that were used in question 1 were repeated in question 2.

The third tolerance section included one item that stated: "Should other children who are caught doing the following things be turned loose, warned and turned over to their parents, put under juvenile court supervision, or sent to jail or a juvenile facility?" Again, this question addressed social control and tolerance issues related to the nine behavioral events.

The fourth and final section asked the respondent to indicate what he or she felt could be done about the amount of delinquency. This section contained 12 items: six covering prevention or prevention strategies, and six related to methods of control (see Appendix A). The 12 items were re-phrased statements of recommendations presented in the reports issued by the President's Commission on Law Enforcement and the Administration of Justice, *The Challenge of Crime in a Free Society*, and *Law and Order Recommendations*, respectively. All items in this section required a yes or no answer.

Likert Scale Codes

All tolerance related questions were treated as Likert-scale items. Section 1 questions were coded on a three point scale (respondent felt the behavior was delinquent (wrong), 3; no response, 2; respondent felt the behavior was not delinquent, 1). For section 2 questions, a five category scale was used (respondent would do nothing, 1; respondent would take personal action, intervening to protect himself or herself and others in the future, 2; no response, 3; respondent would report the behavior to the juvenile's parents or teachers, 4; respondent would report the behavior to the police or other higher authority, 5). The nine behavior items in section 3 were also codes as a five dimension scale (respondent felt that juveniles caught in such behavior should be turned loose, 1; respondent felt that juveniles caught in such behavior should be warned and turned over to their parents, 2; no response, 3; respondent felt that juveniles caught in such behavior should be placed under juvenile court supervision, 4; respondent felt that juveniles caught in such behavior should be sent away to an institution, 5). The final section examined responses to 12 items that dealt with prevention and control. Each item was score as follows (respondent believed this action would help control delinquency, 3; no response, 2; respondent did not believe that the stated action would help control delinquency, 1).

Defining and Measuring Race

Race is difficult to define satisfactorily. Daniel Georges-Abeyie (1984) asserted that "there is no single universally accepted definition of race." He is supported in this view by anthropologists, sociologists, historians and criminologists (Lynch, 2000). Evidence from the GENOME project also has supported that the groups of people we define as belonging to different races are not significantly different genetically. Despite academic views on this matter, Webster's *New Collegiate Dictionary* (1976) defines race as "a family, tribe, people, or nation belonging to the same stock, or a division of mankind possessing traits that are transmissible by descent and sufficient to characterize it as a distinct human type." And, in dated sociological textbooks, race has sometimes been defined as "a subgroup of the human species characterized by physical differences which result from inherited biological characteristics" (Popenoe, 1974), or "a human group that defines itself and/or is defined by other groups as different by virtue of innate and immutable physical characteristics" (Smith & Preston, 1977).

Whether or not races exist in the biological sense, they exist socially. Many types of behaviors have been described as varying by a persons ascribed or sociologically constructed race. Variations in crime, for example, are often examined relative to the race of offenders and victims. As an example, consider Coramae Richey Mann's (1986:38, 39, 285) summary of Black participation in crime extracted from the Uniform Crime Report:

> In sum, although there is an obvious disproportionate involvement of African Americans in official arrest statistics compared with Euro-Americans and other minorities, with the exception of larceny-theft, the types of crimes in which blacks, for example, are involved for the most part tend to reflect vague offenses peculiar to each jurisdiction ("all other offenses"), offenses against the public order (drugs, disorderly conduct, driving under the influence), or violent offenses most commonly committed against other blacks (other assaults, aggravated assault).

It is Mann's (1993) position that "minority status notwithstanding, persons are arrested in this country for essentially the same crimes . . . and a look at each or within each subgroup's arrest portfolio has demonstrated that the proportions of each type of crime do not vary substantially between minorities, or between minorities and whites."

Other authors and researchers define race differently. Walker, Spohn, and Delone (1966), for example, thought that "race and ethnicity are extremely complex and controversial subjects . . . that the categories we use are problematic and do not necessarily reflect the reality of American life." Traditionally, however, the authors maintained that race is referred to as the "major biological divisions of mankind," which are "distinguished by color of skin, color and texture of hair, bodily proportions, and other physical features which identified three major racial groups: Caucasian, Negroid, and Mongoloid." It is the authors' position that scientists have not been able to determine meaningful differences between people who are referred to as white, black, and Asian; especially because migration (human), intermarriages, and evolution has caused intermingling of various people. Yinger (1990) states that "we cannot accept the widespread belief that there are a few clearly distinct and nearly immutable races. Change and intermixture are continuous."

Walker et al. (1996) asserted that anthropologists and sociologists regard the concept of race as "primarily a social construct . . . groups are labeled by both themselves and other groups . . . the politically and culturally dominant group in any society generally defines the labels that are applied to other groups . . . ." Racial designations, the authors remind us, have changed over both political power and racial attitudes. Yinger (1990) notes that the critical categories for social analysis are the "socially visible 'racial' lines based on beliefs about race and on administrative and political classifications rather than genetic differences."

In contrast, in *The Bell Curve*, Richard J. Herrnstein and Charles Murray (1994) argued that success in life is determined largely by IQ, which is inherited and varies between races. The authors indicated that African-Americans consistently scored lower than European-Americans and Asian-Americans in IQ studies. However, critics argue that IQ tests were not a valid measure of intellectual capacity (see Jacoby, Russell, and Glauberman, 1995;

Kamin, 1986; Perkins, 1995).

Despite these problems, measures of race have been defined by the Federal Office of Management and Budget (OMB, 1996). OMB defines a white person as anyone "having origins in any of the original peoples of Europe, North Africa, or the Middle East." It defines a black person as anyone "having origins in any of the black racial groups of Africa" . This seems to mean that a person from Algeria, Egypt, Morocco, or Syria and Iran is classified as "white," while a person from Ghana, Benin Republic, Niger, Nigeria, or Tanzania is classified as "black." So the term "white" is just as inaccurate as "black."

The quality of criminal justice data may very well be lacking because the official data reported by criminal justice agencies are not reliably dependable; criminal justice agencies may not and do not always use the same racial and ethnic categories that would have narrowed the gap between whites and blacks and understate the real effect of racial disparities in arrests (for example, the use of whites, non-whites, Hispanics, and non-Hispanic whites).

While criminologists may not agree about the meaning or definition of race, measures of race have consistently been employed in criminological research. The results have not always been consistent. Spohn et al. (1996) reported that "early self-report studies, those conducted before 1980, found little differences in delinquency rates across race (African-American and White only). Later, more refined self-report designs have produced results that challenge the initial assumption of similar patterns of delinquency." Some research findings, the authors maintained, indicate that African-American males are more likely than white males to report serious criminal behavior (prevalence). Moreover, a larger portion of African-Americans than whites report a high frequency of serious delinquency (incidence).

Huizinga and Elliot (1991) analyzed national youth survey data relating to race-and-prevalence and race-and-incidence. Contrary to Hindelang (1978), they suggest that the differential selection bias hypothesis cannot be readily dismissed, as the differential presence of youth in the criminal justice system cannot be explained entirely by differential offending rates.

Leonard and Sontheimer (1995) tell us that "A number of recent studies have identified race as predictive of juvenile court dispositions, even after controlling for relevant legal criteria: prior record, offense seriousness, type, and level of inquiry or damage. . . Other researchers have reported little or no race effect." The authors also indicated that recent research efforts resulted in inconclusive findings in part due to methodological faults and lack of replication efforts.

Despite these conclusions, race remains a persistent variable used to predict variations in crime and delinquency.

Before turning to a presentation of the data, it is necessary to comment on the procedure used to evaluate the data. These comments concern the use of substantive and statistical methods of evaluating the significance of data.

The Significance of Significance

Any intellectual research or inquiry, whether empirical or otherwise, is an investigation that is initiated within an intellectual frame of reference that influences the interpretation of data (Groves, 1993). Data are often described as objective. Data, however, have no meaning independent of the theoretical lens through which it is observed (Groves, 1993). Thus, great care must be taken when interpreting the meaning of data.

A variety of statistical representations may be employed to make sense of, or interpret data. Statistical significance is one example of a widely used form of statistical representation of data. As a result of the type of data generated in this study, and the nature of the explanation being tested, it was determined that the most plausible method to reveal the findings would be substantive differences observed across race and gender grouped responses.

You are referred to chapter four for a detail explanation and description of the data set including the population, data sources, design, sampling procedure, sample representativeness, etc.

Substantive significance or difference, also referred to as practical or analytic significance, is defined in most introductory statistic book as the importance or meaningfulness of a finding from a practical standpoint. In this chapter, we will be examining the meaningful difference of each group's responses to survey questions regarding delinquency tolerance for the two dimensions of tolerance. In order to evaluate substantive differences, it is still necessary to specify a degree of difference between measures that can be employed as an indicator of difference. For purposes of the current analyses, a difference of 20 percent across groups on each item was taken as an indicator of substantive difference.

The interest in substantive or analytical significance of estimated coefficients has been employed in contemporary criminological research. Deirdre McCloskey (1998) tells us that "the interest in substantive significance is partly due to the inability of statistical significant test to provide researchers with information on the probability that coefficients estimated from a random sample are a matter of chance ... Statistical significance provides us with no information on analytical importance of the coefficients." McCloskey continues this argument, asserting that "no finding of fit or statistical significance testifies in itself to the scientific importance of an effect...fit and importance are not the same thing... Nor is fit something that you first determine, and then move to substance....the substance of an effect is, to use a technical term, its OOMPH...OOMPH ordinarily has nothing whatever to do with whether the coefficient is statistically significant at the different confident levels" (1998). Laurie G. Dodge (2003, p. 180) argues that effect size (practical significance) may be more meaningful in some cases (e.g., large samples; significance tests affected by sample size) than measures of statistical significance. She suggests that it is inappropriate to assume that a statistically significant relationship also has a sizeable effect on an outcome. In fact, a weak or statistically small difference or relationship can have practical or substantive significance. Deirdre Abraham Wald (1939, p. 302), regarded as a pioneer of theoretical statistics tells us that "the question as to how the form of the weight (that is loss or error) function should be determined, is not a mathematical or statistical one…the statistician who wants to test certain hypothesis must first determine the relative importance of all possible errors which will depend on special purpose of his/her investigation".

To be sure, both statistical significance and substantive significance have an important role to play in evaluating theory, and the importance of the statistical significance of effects should not be minimized. For the present study, however, it was determined that substantive significance was an appropriate method for measuring the potential importance of attitudes toward crime or tolerance of crime as these attitudes affect participation in crime. In addition, because this dissertation revolves around an effort to determine if tolerance may help explain crime and does not seek to generalize conclusions from this research, substantive significance is a more appropriate method of assessment.

Tolerance Analysis

The analysis of tolerance employed in this dissertation will, as noted above, rely on distinguishing substantive differences in tolerance of delinquency across groups. In order to establish whether or not the discussion of tolerance laid out in this dissertation may have relevance to explaining patterns of delinquency or crime, two basic group comparisons were made. The first was across gender groups (male vs. female). The second was across racial groups (black vs. white). These groups were selected because of the differences that exist in crime across these groups. For example, the gap in criminal offending between males and females is quite large across a number of more serious offenses, but smaller, or even reversed with respect to less serious offenses. Thus, if tolerance is related to criminal offending, we would expect that females would be less tolerant of serious delinquent acts than males. With respect to race, we would expect to see a persistent pattern of less tolerance among whites compared to blacks, perhaps with a few exceptions (e.g., drug related offenses).

CHAPTER 5 REVIEW QUESTIONS

1. Describe the research method used by the author in the study of delinquency tolerance
2. What does the author mean by significance of significance?
3. What other methods are available to study delinquency tolerance? Explain.

CHAPTER **6**

Results

This chapter presents the results of the data analysis assessing the relationship between attitudes towards delinquents by juveniles and whether or not juveniles also would take action against those acts. As noted previously, those who find delinquency offensive *and* also react to delinquent acts in a manner that upholds their evaluations of delinquent behavior (e.g., report a behavior to police) show concordance between actions and behaviors. It is this group which is defined as not tolerating delinquency.

Tolerance scores by gender and race were constructed for each of the fifteen offenses. Gender tolerance data and scores are presented in Table 5.1. Race-related tolerance data and scores can be found in Table 5.2. The following describes the data found in these Tables.

Summary of Table Contents

Column 1 contains the percentage of the total sample that identified a behavior as wrong. Column 2 contains the percentage of the sample that stated that they would not respond, in any legitimate way (e.g., report the behavior to someone in authority; taking personal, self-protective action was counted as a "non-response"), if they witnessed a specific behavior. The percentage in columns 1 and 2 were multiplied to create the tolerance score for the sample. This result is shown in column 7.

Columns 3 through 6 in each Table show the percentage of the sample that identified a behavior as wrong, and the percentage of the sample that would not respond in a legitimate way if they witnessed a specific behavior for sub-groups. In Table 5.1, the sub-groups are males and females. In Table 5.2 these subgroups are blacks and whites. Columns 8 and 9 contain the tolerance score for each sub-group. In Table 5.1, column 8 shows the tolerance score for males, while column 9 contains the tolerance score for females. In Table 5.2, columns 8 and 9 represent the white and black tolerance scores, respectively. Column 10 presents the difference between the sub-group tolerance scores. A negative score for this measure in Table 5.1 indicates that females were more tolerant of a specific behavior than were males. In Table 5.2, a negative score indicates that whites were more tolerant of a behavior than were blacks. Finally, column 11 in both Tables shows the percentage difference between sub-group's tolerance scores. For male-female sub-groups, the percentage difference was calculated by dividing the male-female tolerance difference (column 11) by the female tolerance score for each offense. Thus, the percentage difference is always measured relative to female tolerance. In Table 5.2, the percentage difference was calculated by dividing the black-white tolerance difference by the black tolerance score for each offense.

The percentage difference scores found in column 11 were used to determine if there was a substantive difference between the subgroups in each case. A twenty-percent difference was selected as the criteria to determine substantive difference.

Males versus Female Tolerance Differences

Employing the twenty percent criteria, it is evident that males and

females were substantively different in only 3 of the fifteen behaviors: talking back to a teacher; cutting someone with a knife;
and breaking and entering a house. The negative tolerance difference score for "talking back to a teacher" indicates that females
were more tolerant of this behavior than males. The positive tolerance difference scores for the remaining two offense categories
indicate that males were more tolerant of these more serious behaviors than females. While the results for these three offenses
fit the hypothesized relationship between gender and tolerance
(males would be more tolerant of deviance, especially more serious acts of deviance, compared to females), overall the data in
Table 5.1 fails to support the hypothesize gender relationship with
tolerance. While four other offense categories come close to the
required substantive significance level selected (talking back to
parents, 17%; shoplifting, 15%; selling drugs, 16%; and having
a gun, 17%), and all are consistent with the expected directional
effects (females are more tolerant than males of less serious offenses; males are more tolerant of serious offenses than females),
even with the addition of these four offenses, males and females
would only be different on 7 of the fifteen offenses, or in less
than one-half of the offenses measured. It should be pointed out
that the lack of a gendered difference cannot be generalized beyond these data given the sampling restrictions encountered while
undertaking this research. However, these data do not provide
support for the theoretical contention that tolerance of delinquency would differ across genders. In effect, this means that we must
reject, at least for these data, the idea that differences in level of
tolerance of deviance might be useful for explaining gendered
differences in offending.

Black versus White Tolerance Differences

For table 5.2, the percentage difference was calculated by dividing
the black-white tolerance difference by the black tolerance score

for each offense. Therefore, the percentage difference scores located in column (11) eleven is used to determine if there was a substantive difference between the subgroups/ black and white in each case.

Applying the twenty percent standard, it is obvious that there is substantive difference between black and white responses in all fifteen of the response categories. Only three of these categories fail to reach the level of substantive difference employed here: cut someone with a knife, ride bike across yard and stay out late. The results are consistent with the directional prediction that black juveniles will be more tolerant of delinquency than are white juveniles.

Unlike the relationship between gender and tolerance, the relationship between race and tolerance appears to hold some potential for explaining participation in delinquency. Indeed, while gender-linked differences were typically small and inconsistent in terms of the direction of the relationship (i.e., in some cases, females were more tolerant of delinquency), race-linked tolerance difference were quite large and consistent in direction. In all cases, black juveniles were more tolerant of delinquent acts than white juveniles. Extremely large race differences were noted for tolerance related to "have a gun" (61%), "sell drugs" (55%) "destroy property" (45.5%), "shoplifting" (40.5%), "talkback to parent" (39%), "talkback to teacher" (38%), "swear at teacher" (37%), "break and enter a house" (33.5%), and "smoke marihuana" (31%), or on 9 of the 15 items. Thus, not only is there a race difference with respect to tolerance, the race differences that exist are fairly substantial. Further, it should be noted that the race differences indicated in Table 5.2 do not appear to be correlated with the seriousness of the offense. For example, race differences were very high for minor offenses such as talking back to parents or teachers, but low for other minor offenses such as riding a bike across someone's yard, or staying out late. Likewise, race differences for serious offenses show some inconsistency. While the largest race difference shown in Table 5.2 exist for one the most serious offense, have a gun (61%), much smaller race differences are found for another serious offense, cut someone with a knife (13.5%). Thus, it would appear that race differences can not be explained with reference to offense seriousness.

Conclusion

The data analysis employed substantive differences to assess whether juvenile tolerance of delinquent acts varied by gender and race. Substantive and persistent differences were found for race. These findings indicate that race-linked tolerance of delinquency difference may help explain differential participation in delinquency across race groups.

No persistent gender-related tolerance differences were found across the fifteen items used in this research. Thus, while race appears to be useful for explaining delinquency participation through tolerance of delinquent acts, the same conclusion cannot be reach with respect to gender. The implications of these findings are discussed more fully on the following chapter.

CHAPTER 6 REVIEW QUESTIONS

1. Are there differential adolescent delinquency tolerance? If so, explain.
2. Discuss and interpret the tables in this chapter

Table 5.1:
Delinquency Tolerance (Attitudes and Responses), Gender Comparisons Across Fifteen Different Offenses

Questions	(1) M+F Wrong	(2) M+F Non Rep.	(3) Male Wrong	(4) Male Non Rep.	(5) Female Wrong	(6) Female Non Rep.	(7) M+F Tolerance	(8) Male Tolerance	(9) Female Tolerance	(10) M-F Tolerance Difference	(11) F-M Percent Difference
Talkback Teacher	.759	.341	.747	.307	.802	.373	.259	.229	.299	-.07	23
Swear at Teacher	.787	.34	.783	.334	.821	.338	.268	.262	.277	-.015	5
Talkback Parent	.764	.453	.743	.427	.817	.469	.346	.317	.383	-.066	17
Swear at Parent	.866	.411	.84	.394	.901	.425	.356	.331	.383	-.052	13.5
Fight with Juvenile	.822	.36	.823	.373	.833	.330	.296	.307	.275	.032	11.5
Cut someone with a Knife	.893	.324	.863	.346	.937	.265	.289	.299	.248	.051	20.5
Bike Across someone's yard	.764	.417	.783	.393	.742	.433	.319	.308	.321	-.013	4
Shoplift	.917	.296	.88	.320	.964	.254	.271	.282	.245	.037	15
Break and enter a house	.949	.319	.923	.337	.980	.262	.303	.311	.257	.054	21

TABLE 5.1 ⟩

	(1)	(2)	(3)	(4)	(5)	(6)	(7)	(8)	(9)	(10)	(11)
Destroy Property	.852	.278	.847	.290	.877	.250	.237	.246	.219	.027	12
Stay out Late	.715	.433	.737	.410	.683	.453	.310	.302	.309	-.007	2
Turn in a False Alarm	.894	.364	.873	.364	.917	.334	.325	.318	.306	.012	4
Sell drugs	.921	.238	.893	.257	.960	.207	.219	.230	.199	.031	16
Have a gun	.843	.229	.833	.246	.881	.199	.193	.205	.175	.030	17
Smoke Marijuana	.868	.327	.86	.330	.885	.306	.284	.284	.271	.013	5

1. Percentage of the total sample (males and females) who state the behavior is wrong.
2. Percentage of the total sample (males and females) who would not take any action.
3. Percentage of the males who state the behavior is wrong.
4. Percentage of the males who would not take any action.
5. Percentage of the females who state the behavior is wrong.
6. Percentage of the females who would not take any action.
7. Tolerance score for the entire sample (1 * 2)
8. Tolerance score for males (3 * 4).
9. Tolerance score for females (5 * 6).
10. Difference between the tolerance score for males and females. Negative scores indicate that males are less tolerant of a given behavior than females (8 – 9).
11. Percentage difference between male and female tolerance score. ([[(9 – 8)/9)]* 100).

TABLE 5.2 ❯

Table 5.2:

Delinquency Tolerance (Attitudes and Responses), Race Comparisons Across Fifteen Different Offenses

Questions	(1) B+W Wrong	(2) B+W Non Rep.	(3) White Wrong	(4) White Non Rep.	(5) Black Wrong	(6) Black Non Rep.	(7) B+W Tolerance	(8) White Tolerance	(9) Black Tolerance	(10) B-W Tolerance Difference	(11) B-W Percent Difference
Talkback Teacher	.759	.341	.707	.288	.762	.435	.259	.204	.331	.127	38
Swear Teacher	.787	.34	.767	.271	.745	.444	.340	.208	.331	.123	37
Talkback Parent	.764	.453	.694	.396	.795	.569	.346	.275	.452	.177	39
Swear Parent	.866	.411	.866	.362	.841	.506	.356	.313	.426	.113	26.5
Fight with Juvenile	.822	.36	.871	.301	.745	.481	.296	.262	.358	.096	27
Cut some-one with a knife	.893	.324	.884	.380	.883	.440	.289	.336	.389	.053	13.5
Ride bike across yard	.764	.417	.776	.401	.753	.502	.319	.311	.378	.067	18
Shoplifting	.917	.296	.931	.242	.895	.423	.271	.225	.379	.154	40.5

	(1)	(2)	(3)	(4)	(5)	(6)	(7)	(8)	(9)	(10)	(11)
Break and enter a house	.949	.319	.957	.271	.941	.414	.303	.259	.390	.131	33.5
Destroy Property	.852	.278	.832	.216	.841	.393	.237	.180	.331	.151	45.5
Stay out late	.715	.433	.754	.401	.661	.544	.310	.302	.360	.058	16
Turn in a false alarm	.894	.364	.922	.306	.858	.471	.325	.282	.404	.122	30
Sell drugs	.921	.238	.922	.159	.912	.356	.219	.147	.325	.178	55
Have a gun	.843	.229	.828	.142	.824	.364	.193	.118	.300	.182	61
Smoke Marihuana	.868	.327	.892	.280	.845	.431	.284	.250	.364	.114	31

TABLE 5.2 ➤

1. Percentage of the total sample (black and white) who state the behavior is wrong.
2. Percentage of the total sample (black and white) who would not take any action.
3. Percentage of whites who state the behavior is wrong.
4. Percentage of whites who would not take any action.
5. Percentage of blacks who state the behavior is wrong.
6. Percentage of blacks who would not take any action.
7. Tolerance score for the entire sample (1 * 2)
8. Tolerance score for whites (3 * 4).
9. Tolerance score for blacks (5 * 6).
10. Difference between the tolerance score for blacks and whites. Negative scores indicate that blacks are less tolerant of a given behavior than blacks (8 − 9).
11. Percentage difference between black and white tolerance score. ([[(9 − 8)/9)]* 100).

Discussion and Conclusions

The hypotheses of this study revolved around delinquency toler-ance. It was postulated that there would be a differential in the tolerance of delinquent behavior by juveniles from different gen-der and racial groups. That is, it was hypothesized that different groups would score higher or lower on select measures of delin-quency tolerance.

Theoretically, tolerance involves differential attitudes of various subgroups toward the violations of norms relating to acceptable behavior by juveniles. Tolerance may vary across both individu-als and groups. Variability of tolerance can be considerable from group to group and across individuals.

The design of the study entailed the use of the self-report/ opinion technique of data collection. Using this technique, the researcher obtained permission from the county schools' adminis-tration for access to various public schools, and from parents. The data were collected under direction of Professor Fredrick Faust, a faculty member in the School of Criminology at Florida State University. The research design was approved by the Board of Research at Florida State University and the Leon County School Board. Participation was voluntary on behalf of students, parents and teachers. Each participant was presented with a questionnaire in a pre-selected class. The total survey sample was 562. The questionnaire was constructed in a manner to facilitate the analysis of each of the tolerance dimensions separately. The questionnaire also elicited information regarding respondents' characteristics (i.e., education, number of siblings, trouble with police, trouble with teachers, trouble with parents, trouble with school).

The major hypotheses of this study were:

1. Black juveniles are more tolerant of delinquency than white juveniles.
2. Juvenile boys will be more tolerant of delinquency than juvenile girls.

The data were analyzed by analysis of variance of group mean scores and subsequent substantive difference/significance. Hypothesis 1 was supported while hypothesis 2 was rejected.

In view of the fact that very little related research could be found with respect to delinquency tolerance, it is felt that this study breaks new ground. But, what implications do the results of the current research hold? And what limitations where inherent in this research?

First, it should be made clear that the results of this study are specifically applicable only to a limited population in a given geographic location. As a result, it would not be appropriate to state the findings in terms of broad generalizations or universal conclusions. Second, the survey was written at a 5th grade reading level. Surveys were, however, distributed to youth who were either under the age usually attained by 5th graders, or whose reading levels were not assessed. This could affect the results of the study. Third, the questions for the survey were adapted from previous research on adults. The changes made to previous adult-specific surveys were designed to elicit responses from youth to behaviors they were likely to encounter, and which represented a range a behaviors. The behaviors this research focused on are not the only possible behaviors, thus limiting the generality of the empirical analysis. Fourth, because of the complexities involved in obtaining a sample of under-aged youth in schools, the design that emerged use a non-random sample, threatening the validity of the results. In today's environment, however, it is becoming more difficult to obtain random samples from schools, and researchers should keep this issue in mind before starting their research. Fifth, other factors known to correlate with delinquency, such as social class and age, were either not included as a variable in this investigation (social class), or omitted because of sample size issues (age). Future research could address these omissions. Finally, the survey asked youth about their attitudes, and what they might do when confronted with such behavior. It did not, however, investigate the behaviors in which these youth actually participated. Research on this issue, it was felt, was better left to the future after the initial aspects of the theory had been tested.

Despite these limitations, the sample that resulted was statistically similar to the population of youth in the school system under examination. Consequently, these finding may be useful for offering observations about the further development of criminological explanations or theories may be derived.

To summarize, the major findings of this study were as follows:

1. Males were slightly more tolerant of delinquent behavior than females were. The gender-related tolerance hypothesis was, however, rejected, given that gender differences were small and inconsistent.
2. Blacks were more tolerant of delinquent behavior than were whites. This hypothesis was accepted.
3. In terms of how delinquency is defined and reported, blacks were more tolerant of delinquent behavior.
4. For correction or intervention, there was no significant difference between males or females. There was no significant difference among the races in this dimension of tolerance.

Making Sense of the Findings

In the introduction to this dissertation, it was stated that the theoretical basis of the study was influenced by the idea that the normative limits of deviant and conforming behavior were affected by an individual's level of delinquency tolerance, which, in turn was impacted by tolerance levels associated with group norms (race and gender). Consistent with this view, it was assumed that tolerance of delinquency would vary with participation in delinquency. Given that the most persistent finding involved race, a logical explanation of this relationship is required. Reasonable explanations for this relationship may be found in the nature of community, family, or social welfare organization and socialization.

Evidence demonstrates that adolescents living in hardships and deprived environments may be exposed to certain aspects of urban life that may be deleterious to their wellbeing. We suggest that tolerance of delinquency may be the available avenue for certain adolescents to navigate their economically, socially, and politically deprived communities. African Americans are concentrated in environments that are characterized by this phenomenon. Their situation is even exacerbated by individual and institutional discrimination, restriction of access to power and structural changes that render them poor and disillusioned. The environment is characterized by high unemployment, inadequate education and housing, family disruption and crime and delinquency tolerance and violence. By adolescence, many African Americans become aware of their social disadvantages through experience and or observation. This experience may generate feelings of powerlessness and lead to despair and frustration, anger and aggression and tolerance of delinquency. Many Black adolescents relegated to families embedded in criminogenic areas and without economic or social-political resources. They are not encouraged to participate in support activities that place adolescents in healthy and monitored environments where they may be exposed to behavioral alternatives.

Self-Control and Self-Concept

The general theory of crime and delinquency is a refined version of control theory that focuses on control through social bonds and a specific concept referred to as self-concept. It is the position of researchers who support this view that we need to emphasize and separate crime from criminality. Individuals who have low self-concept or control tend to get involved in criminal transactions and in this case are more tolerant of delinquent behavior. Low self control may result from several different processes. In the view of Gottfredson and Hirschi, it is most likely the result of inadequate child-rearing practices. This assertion is based on their argument that self-control is essentially stable across time. For example, they argue that by age eight an individual's level of self-control has been determined by child-rearing practices of guardians or parents. The authors expanded inadequate the concept of self-control to include measures of behavior such as inability to defer gratifications, absence of a perseverance effort and tenacious, risk-taking behavior, a preference for physical activity over cognition, self-centered perspectives, and very low levels of frustration tolerance. Self- concept can be defined as ideas, feelings, perception and thoughts about the self. The theory relates how we as individuals evaluate the self whether positively or negatively, which determines how we adapt to our social environment. When are unable to achieve a positive self-concept, we levitate towards a concept that may be defined as tolerating deviance in our society.

Consistent with this view, Erikson (1968) held that the main theme of life is the quest for identity. It is his position that throughout life we ask, "who am I?" and form a different answer at each stage of life. Erikson tells us that self-concept it is a dynamic process of testing, selecting, and integrating thoughts and feelings about self and at the end of each stage the person's sense of identity is reconfirmed on a new level. At this point, identity is transformed from one stage to the next, and early forms influence later forms. Erikson argued that adolescents in the midst of identity crises may seek temporary solution in over identifying with some popular hero or with a social group to the extent of identity loss and that this crises is resolved through commitment.

Adolescents who lack commitment are more tolerant of delinquent behavior. African American youths are readily exposed to elevated crime and delinquency rates because of their social status and /or family demography. Research indicates that growing up with values inconsistent with those of the mainstream can be a risk to adolescent delinquency tolerance. Additional analysis (not shown) related to the issue of identity uncovered a curvilinear relationship between age and delinquency tolerance where tolerance of delinquency was lowest among the oldest and youngest age groups. Using the notions self-control and self-concept, it could be argued that the youth in the middle age group who are searching for their identities are more likely than older or younger youth to accept delinquency as part of this process of identity discovery. That is, in searching for their identities, the age group in the middle is more willing to explore and accept delinquent identities than other age groups.

Self-Esteem

Self-esteem is another important component of self-concept. Burchard (1996) in his study of early adolescence concluded that an initial drop in self-esteem may be likely due to change in school, body, etc.,. This stage is referred to as the period of the baritone for boys and other physical development for boys and girls. Furthermore, youths at the early development (12-16) experience a weak sense of individual identity and need for peer validation. This is sometimes referred to as youth social revolution. This is when supervision is critical. Adolescents may begin to develop social habits; make-up for example for girls and smoking and interest in sexual activities for boys. Burchard also found that friendships become sources of self worth and self-esteem, and important in the search for identity. Again, Burchard's explanation helps explain the difference seen in this study across age groups with respect to tolerance of delinquency.

Today's adolescents encounter far more social risks and face far more societal pressure to be successful in most aspect of life than those of previous eras. Hamburg (1993) tells us that "today's adolescents face demands and expectations, as well as risks and temptations, that appear to be more numerous and complex than those adolescents faced a generation ago". Noam (1997) and Weissburg and Greenberg (1997) argued that "the majority of adolescents find the transition from childhood to adulthood a time of physical, cognitive, and social development that provides considerable challenge, opportunities, and growth...too many adolescents today are not provided with adequate opportunity and support to become competent adults...they are provided with less stable environment, high divorce rates, high adolescents pregnancies, increased geographical mobility and exposed to debilitating complex menu of lifestyle options". Thus, faced with such instability, delinquent identities may provide a sense of belonging for some adolescents. For example, research on gangs indicates that youth join gangs to belong to a close social unit and to feel loved and respected by somebody. This was the primary responsibility of the original family unit. Gangs are known to have their own norms which are usually in conflict with the norms of the so-called conventional society. Adolescent period of transition makes them very likely to join gangs to protect their feelings of inadequacy and confusion.

Stages of Development and Tolerance

Piaget (1954) argued that our transition through life goes through four stages in understanding the world and each of the stages are interwoven and consists of particular ways of thinking. Piaget reminded us that it is the different way of understanding the world that makes one stage more advanced and distinct than another. Piaget first stage of cognitive development is the sensorimotor (birth to 2 years) where the infant is believed to construct an understanding of the world by coordinating sensory experience with physical actions. The preoperational stage (2 to 7 years) is where the child begins to represent the world with words and images. The concrete operational stage (7 to 11) is where the child is able to reason logically about concrete events and classify them. The final cognitive stage is the formal operational (11 to 15 or 16). At this stage the adolescent reasons in more abstract and logical ways to the extent that their thoughts are more idealistic. These stages of cognitive development espoused by Piaget deserve a closer examination. It is our position that all four stages are important to understanding adolescent delinquency tolerance. In stage one for example, it will be necessary to be vigilant as the child begins to construct understanding of the environment. If for example the child continue to cry after it is determined that enough food has been consumed, it may be wise not to continue the feeding. This is a way of training the child to be aware of the implications of the action. This training must be consistent throughout the stages and should include every form of action that the guardians deem inconsistent with "normal" behavior. It is necessary that this process or training be progressively stern and consistent.

Kohlberg (1976) argued that full moral development is achieved by progressing through a developmental series of cognitive changes of preconventional, conventional and post-conventional individually divided into early and late substages. Kohlberg believe that stage one and two are dominated by an individualistic and egocentric orientation and the later stages may be dominated by a broader social perspective and behavior directed at gaining approval and more complete conscience development. Kohlberg viewed delinquent adolescents as having their morality held hostage in the first two stages. The non-delinquent adolescents are more likely to have reached stages three and four (Kohlberg, 1973). There is consensus among researchers that delinquents may be predictably characterized by pre-conventional moral thinking than non-delinquents.

The quality of behavior associated with pre-conventional stage is, perhaps, characteristic of the tolerance levels expressed by the 12 to16 year old age group in this study. Arbuthnot, Gordon, and Jurkovic (1987) review of several studies testing Kohlberg's theory found delinquents to perform at a lower cognitive level than non-delinquents. Future research, therefore, should examine whether tolerance levels of 12 to 16 year olds is related to variation in their stage of moral development as well. Based on the social status and family demography of the African American adolescents, it not surprising that this population of youths will have low self-concept, esteem, and identity and will suffer most frustration in stages of development associated with adolescence. For example, Black youths are more likely to live in deprived neighborhoods and research shows that adolescents who are bred in such environment are at increased risk for emotional and behavioral problems that are likely contributors to delinquency tolerance. In such impoverished environment where illegitimate sources of income may be available, it is more economically feasible to violate the norms of society and be tolerant of criminal and delinquent behavior.

Implications

In this section, various implications of the present research are examined. These implications are of three general types: (1) policy;

(2) theory; and (3) research. Implications for each of these areas is discussed below.

Policy

The results of this study have some general implications for the planning of juvenile delinquency programs dealing with correction, prevention, and control. Some suggestions are made here as examples in which inferences may be drawn from the findings of the study that might prove helpful in the planning of specific activities. Though these suggestions should not be taken as the sole reason for program action, they might be helpful in specific program planning.

A comparison of the findings relating to the prevention and control dimensions of delinquency tolerance suggests that females and males and black and white groups, would favor community efforts (i.e., improved living conditions, better housing, jobs for parents, etc.). They also support fair law enforcement and support for more black police officers in black neighborhoods for example.

These few words provide only a general orientation toward policy issues. More will be said about policy in the section "Research and Policy."

Theory

This study was designed within the theoretical framework of normative deviance theory. According to Steinhart (1989), Stalans and Henry, (1994) and several other authors specializing in the study of deviance, it would be impossible to discuss deviance without reference to norms or expectations since normative expectations are the base-line against which deviance must be measured. The normative-deviance approach takes the view that deviance is always defined normatively. It is important to note that the normative order defines and creates the limits of acceptable and unacceptable conduct. In terms of this dissertation, the normative order helps to define the limits of an individual's tolerance for deviance, delinquency and crime. This observation raises several related issues.

First, because crime is an outcome of a political process where conflicting interests sometimes meet, at times law will represent the interests or normative expectations of some, but not all members of a society. Thus, when groups with less tolerance have more power and are in a better position to shape the law, other groups, which are more tolerant of deviance, may be placed in circumstances that enhance the probability that they will violate the law. In other words, while tolerance affects how crime is perceived and defined, power affects the ability of a group to translate their tolerance level into law. These ideas are consistent with the normative approach of Durkheim, the labeling approach, and critical/conflict criminological positions.

The critical or conflict perspective is considered a radical/ Marxist derivative and its view of adolescent delinquency tolerance focuses on the social and political conditions that encourages delinquency tolerance. This view argues that to remove the elements that drive tolerance of delinquency, society must concentrate on changes necessary to dismiss injustice. Conflict theory is grounded in the belief that the American society is demographically characterized by social and physical segregations, polarized by class conflict and a lack of justice. C. M. Sinclair (1990) argued that "law is recognized as a social product and a social force...society is organized through exercise of power by a small but elite ruling class...society is held together by force and constraint...delinquent acts are so defined only because it is in the interest of the ruling class to define them as such". Those whose behavior are incompatible with those of the ruling class are therefore labeled delinquents. That is, the ruling class determines the level of delinquency tolerance based on their normative values. Behavior that is consistent with delinquency tolerance is regarded as a violation of norms and then labeled by a group of observers.

In a similar statement, labeling theorist, Howard Becker (1973) argued that "social groups create deviance by making the rules whose infraction constitute deviance and by applying those rules to particular people and labeling them as outsiders...from this point of view deviance is not a quality of the act the person commits, but rather a consequence of the application by others of rules or sanctions to an offender...the deviant is one to whom that label has been successfully applied; deviant behavior is behavior that people so label". In this view, adolescent delinquency tolerance may be better understood through a relativistic point of view.

Another issue lie in the fact that people are different and adolescents who are members of different race, age and gender group may be exposed to values that conflict with those of the dominant culture. This may make some (especially those who's behaviors are inconsistent with those of the dominant group) segment of adolescent population more susceptible to violating laws reflecting a lower tolerance of delinquency.

According to Durkheim (1897) "there cannot be a society in which the individuals do not differ more or less from the collective type". Durkheim also argued that "crime is normal" in the sense that a collectivity without criminal transactions would be deeply over-policed or controlled. Such societies would have relatively few crimes, but would never be devoid of crime. In contrast to such societies stand those that generate anomie. Alex Thio (2001) argued that by anomie, Durkheim referred "to an absence of social norms, which implies the failure of a society to control its members' behavior through laws, customs, and other norms".

Durkheim (1897) also argued "society cannot be formed without our being required to make perpetual and costly sacrifices." These forfeiture of valued individuality "embodied in the demands of the collective conscience, are the price of membership in society, and fulfilling the demands gives the individual members a sense of collective identity, which is an important source of social solidarity...but, more important, these demands are constructed so that it is inevitable that a certain number of people will not fulfill them" (Vold, Bernard, and Snipes, 2002). From a theoretical vantage point, this argument implies that groups that feel unattached to society because of racial or ethnic biases, or economic and spatial marginalization, may not share in the values of the dominant culture. Consequently, these groups may tend to develop values that are more tolerant of crime and delinquency, or alternative lifestyles and means of earning a livelihood.

Above, tolerance of delinquency was discussed relative to definitional issues and values, and the ability to translate values into laws. But, tolerance may also impact crime by altering the likelihood that someone will decide to engage in deviant behavior, or perceive a behavior as acceptable even though it has been defined as illegitimate by society. In other words, tolerance may help explain factors that motivate criminal behavior. Thus, the idea of tolerance may help extend the explanations of criminal behavior found in several existing theories of crime.

In regards to control theory, the basic tenet is that all men are potential criminals. And when one speaks of social control one is usually referring to governmental bodies such as the police, the courts, corrections and their subsidiary units. There are other types of social control as well. It is these "other types" of social control that are the primary concern of control theory. These other forms of control include organized bodies or agencies like churches, schools, or less organized social formations such as friends, peers, neighbors and significant others. One can differentiate deviance from crime, right from wrong, delinquency from non-delinquency in terms of activities that arouse stigmatization, indignation or similar reaction within one's environment. Unofficial and popular or official attitudes towards delinquency or negative definitions of its tolerance can be a powerful force for juveniles. Control theory tells us that youths who have positive attitudes will resist the temptation of the violation of law. Kaplan (1991) found that youths with poor self concepts are the ones most likely to violate the law and engage in delinquent behavior. So for control theory, people obey the law because behavior and passion are being controlled by internal and external forces. These same forces may control attitudes towards delinquency tolerance, which in turn will diminish the motivation to engage in delinquency.

Cultural deviance theory is a combination of the effects of social disorganization and strain. Members of some group create an independent sub-culture with their own rules and values. Sub-cultural norms are often in opposition or clash with those of conventional values. When this happens, according to Sellin (1938) culture conflict occurs. Members of juvenile racial groups may be socialized within their group. Their values may be in conflict with those of the conventional society. As a result, their attitude toward delinquency may also be different from those of other groups. Cultural deviance theory may in other words, help us understand delinquency tolerance as it relates to a juvenile's racial or ethnic group affiliation. It will specifically help explain why some acts of delinquency may be seen as acceptable by insiders and unacceptable by outsiders, and how motivations to delinquency may develop.

Future Research and Policy

There is no reason to doubt that, when the concept of adolescent delinquency tolerance was first introduced in the major hypotheses of this study no one could have imagined that it could generate future research endeavors that could change the way societies reacts to their adolescents. The study indicates that our adolescents are generally good kids. Thus, the reaction of society in general must be carefully evaluated. Let us look more closely and sincerely at several challenging social and developmental issues facing adolescents today. Adolescent delinquency tolerance cannot be divorced from these social issues. Furthermore, the moral foundation that breeds good character is also threatened by these same phenomena.

Firstly, the physical, physiological and the corresponding cognitive developmental changes involved in "growing up" generate pressures that adolescents experience. It is pertinent that researchers and the society at large pay close attention to these pressures especially as this transition to adulthood impacts delinquency. John Conger in *Adolescent: Generation Under Pressure* (1979 p. 17) argued that

> despite the variations in the way the young are treated in different societies, one aspect of adolescence is universal: the physical and physiological changes of puberty that mark its beginning, and the young person's need to find some way to adjust to and master these changes...no other developmental event is more dramatic nor more challenging... in the few short years of early adolescence, one has to cope with a virtual biological revolution within oneself: rapid growth in height and weight, changing bodily dimensions, hormonal changes leading to increased sex drive, the development of primary and secondary sexual characteristics and further growth of mental ability.

It is Conger's (1979) position that society at large and the more immediate social units of adolescents may impede or encourage positive or negative transition out of this sometimes traumatic adolescence developmental stage. One such transition or turning point is identified by life course research, which takes as its focus the identification of "turning points" in the process of life development. Life course research may help pinpoint periods in youths' lives during which they are especially vulnerable to developing attitudes conducive to the toleration of delinquency.

Charles Scribner (1968, p. 34) in his discussion of the "Universal Tasks of Adolescence" argued that " the adolescent has enforced upon him/her the invariable task of moving from his/her family of origin to a different (his own) family of procreation; to assume adult procreative function, they must sever close ties with the nuclear family and establish them with blood strangers...a change from the to providing nurture...expected to learn how to work and love...withdrawal from parents normally causes a kind of mourning reaction or episodes of depression...in the effort to reconcile his drives with cultural decrees, the adolescent in any culture employs previously developed, identical defense mechanisms such as repression, denial and projection". Each of these transformations and experiences marks important turning points in the life course. Each may also influence attitudes toward the tolerance of delinquency.

Secondly, this society seems to have allowed certain social problems to persist. These social traps help destabilize adolescent normal growth process. The traps include drug use, sex, pregnancy, welfare program, gang, inadequate public school education, violence; they are encountered in the media, at home and in the community. The fact that adults and the village cannot deal with the problem of the consumption of legal and illegal drugs is a crucial social problem of youths. Adolescence is a period of experimentation. Adolescent try to find the best fit for them as they transition through this period. The National Institute on Drug Abuse (2001) announced that by age 14, 35% of youths have engaged in some form of controlled substances and that 5% of 12th graders reported using cocaine in the year 2000. The drug use problem may be activated by poor parent adolescent relationships, interactions with peers who use, high risk or disadvantaged and dysfunctional communities, family members' drug use, low self-worth and school failure. Drugs may be a "gateway" to crime, as some argue, or a turning point. Current research has not, however, definitely established a causal relationship between the two. Future research may also explore the drug-delinquency-crime connection by addressing whether youth who use drugs and turn to delinquency and crime are also those who are most tolerant of these activities.

Society also exposes adolescents to an enticing blitz of violence especially in the media and internet and also at home and in the community. Today, many adolescents are unsupervised by their rightful guardians who may legitimately be doing constructive work for society to provide for the family. The fact is that the adolescents are unsupervised and they will find something to do. They are at the stage where imitating both actions and expression is common. Does exposure to media affect delinquency? And does this process work by making youth more tolerant of violence and crime? These are questions future research may address. Does the possible connection between media exposure and delinquency call for further legislation controlling the content and time of broadcast of certain shows and enhanced labeling of DVDs, video tapes, and video games? Without speculating on this possibility, we can certain postulate that some one will entertain these ideas as valid policy responses to the problem of crime and delinquency in our society.

Another important factor that is so appalling a social challenge for adolescents is the prison industry's active recruitment and adulteration of our youths. This may be the most shameless industry of our time. The prison industry has very powerful lobbyists who are able to pressure congress to pass legislations favorable and profitable to their industry. Some of these legislations such Zero-tolerance for drug possession, three strikes and you are out, and the recent Zero-tolerance on public school grounds are driven by a bogus political and economic get tough on crime policies that are designed to derail the smooth transition of adolescence to adulthood. The situation is driven by pure greed, greed that ignores the impact of the policy. Unfortunately, the current policy of Zero-tolerance in the public school for example is punitive and does not encourage moral education or communication between adults/teachers and adolescents that may lead to less tolerance of delinquency. This policy has nothing more than a relentless, dangerous, desperate, and deliberate pursuit of humans especially adolescents as commodity for the sole purpose of enhancing and sustaining the financial viability of the prison industry. We also need to begin examining what I have dubbed 'pharmaco-social friction'. This term describes the plight of adolescents when society allow them access to legal or illegal drugs, alcohol and nicotine and prohibit them from participating in activities associated with the consumption of those substances.

Finally, we need to revisit some of the vague definitions of delinquency such incorrigibility, waywardness, and other status offenses that encourages net-widening. These definitions allow some juvenile court jurisdictions to trap certain segment of adolescent population in the criminal/juvenile justice system. These definitions may be especially problematic for the minority groups whose way of life is in conflict with the so-called conventional society.

Back to Durkheim

The issue that is most disturbing and that may have activated adolescent delinquency tolerance is the inadequate moral education of children in schools, in the communities and within the family unit. Society has removed the most powerful pacifying agent from the public school system -- religion. It is my contention that moral education can prevent adolescent tolerant of delinquent behavior.

Though moral development and education of our youths is a controversial issue, it is an area that criminological researchers need to begin to revisit. Piaget, like Durkheim, believed moral development was a natural result of attachment to a group, and many contemporary criminologists continue to investigate the association between attachment and crime. This attachment according to the authors manifests itself in a respect for the group symbols, rules and authority. Michael Braswell (2000, p. 9) asked "how do we attempt to transform the energy of negative, destructive relationships into positive ones? We do it through working on ourselves...through our own attitudes as correctional counselors and other treatment professionals. We cannot give inmates an attitude or values we do not have". This is very true of adolescent delinquency tolerance. How can adults and the village respond to delinquency tolerance if they themselves show tolerance to delinquent and other criminal behavior? Lozoff (1985:398) tell us that

> a staff person who's calm and strong and happy is worth his or her weight in gold. People who are living examples of truthfulness, good humor, patience, and courage are going to change more lives...even if they are employed as janitors than the counselors who cannot get their own lives in order." Braswell argued that effective correctional relationships are centered on respecting where the other is currently and potentially can be...an attempt is made not to focus on how in this case adolescents ought to be but rather on how they are and what they can become. Moral strength in a relationship requires that adults look deep within themselves and their relationships with their children for the healing value of positive social interactions so that we can restore the best moral quality and credibility of our relationships with adolescents.

Ba (1980), a Senegalese writer in 'So Long a Letter' writes "Each profession, intellectual or manual, deserves consideration, whether it requires painful physical effort or manual dexterity, wide knowledge or the patience of an ant...ours, like that of the doctor, does not allow for any...you don't joke with life, and life is both body and mind...to warp a soul is much a sacrilege as murder... teachers and –at kindergarten level, as at university level-form a noble army accomplishing daily feats, never praised, never decorated...an army forever on the move, forever vigilant...an army without drums, without gleaming uniforms...this army, thwarting traps and snares, everywhere plants the flag of knowledge and morality". Adults and the village can and must endeavor to improve moral strength to deal with the problem of adolescent delinquency tolerance. In order to be successful, we must communicate openly with our youths. Let us listen, hear them and take their suggestions into consideration.

In the early 20th century, Emile Durkheim wrote in "Moral Education" (1961) that,

> No doubt God continues to play an important part in morality. It is He who assures respect for it and represses its violation. Offenses against Him... moral discipline was not instituted for His benefit, but for the benefit of men. He only intervenes to make it effective...but if we methodologically reject the notion of the sacred without systematically replacing it by another, the quasi-religious character of morality is without foundation since we are rejecting the traditional conception that provided that foundation without providing another.

To strengthen morality in our communities and in our schools such that adolescents can drink from this fountain of moral education, we cannot afford not to improve this same morality.

Future Research

This study can be seen as contributing to a foundation for future research that will seek to investigate the relevance of delinquency tolerance to research, theory and policy. Future research should generate more interests in the area of delinquency tolerance that has been ignored far too long. There is a need to develop study that focus on social economic status and tolerance of delinquency. Further inquiry into whether there is clear co-variation between delinquency tolerance and age, gender and race is necessary. It is suggested that further research should explore and question the effectiveness of explanatory authority of current theories of delinquency that neglected tolerance of delinquency.

Conclusion

The dissertation was a quest to investigate adolescent attitudes toward delinquent behavior and to determine whether there is differential adolescent tolerance of delinquency race and gender groups, because these attributes have been demonstrated to be persistent correlates of delinquency. The results of this study indicate that there is a differential adolescent tolerance of delinquent behavior among certain groups.

This study raises a widely held belief: that differential attitudes toward delinquency displayed by adolescents reflects a lack of moral strength of adults in the family and other social institutions. For adolescents to exhibit such a nonchalant attitude toward delinquency tolerance demands a reexamination of society's code of conduct. Are we establishing an useful code of conduct for our youths? Is the society or our youths too sophisticated for the prevailing code of conduct today? Should the society raise or lower the code of the conduct bar? How can adults and the society at large or the village enhance and stimulate their moral strength to the extent that it attracts adolescents?

Moral education can be a stout strategy for prevention of delinquency tolerance. The age of first contact with law enforcement is declining and the society seems to be hardening their hearts toward juveniles. The strategy will continue to fail as is apparent in youthful misconduct and violence.

How does society help build moral conduct? One mechanism might be through an increase in the number of religious programs, a strategy which was not approved by Durkheim. More than this, a comprehensive, cooperative and multi-institutional efforts is a necessity. The emphasis however has to be both a parental and societal responsibility for a complete education which must include moral education. The purpose of moral education is to nurture morality as a both virtue and a foundation on which adolescents can build a disciplined approach to life. Since education is one of society's cultural goals and part of the process of character formation, the cultural portion of moral education must be included as part of the system of public education. The strategy is the development of prevention policies founded upon moral strength that will elevate and empower adolescents to challenge the tolerance of delinquent behavior.

Based on the above evaluation and analysis of relevant literature and the substantive difference results, we are able to conclude that the theory of delinquency tolerance states that there are variations in delinquency tolerance amongst adolescent race and gender groups. The theory is guided by the following assumptions: (1). There is a differential adolescent tolerance of delinquency among racial and gender groups. (2). These variations can be found among intimate groups such as family, peers, classmates, communities etc. (3). Differential socialization is a direct effect of delinquency tolerance. (4). Adolescents who are not adequately socialized based on the norms of the conventional society will be more tolerant of delinquency. (5). Need and risk factors such as quality of life, economic security/insecurity, anomie, developmental frustrations, parents/guardians social status and quality of life, prevailing political and economic system, the relation to the system, and perception of the social structure including the criminal/juvenile justice system are vital to the explanation of delinquency tolerance. (6). Desensitivity to violent norms- because of the continuing exposure to violent norms, adolescent become desensitized to delinquency tolerance; they internalize these norms and the norms are reinforced with the norm language. Once this is accomplished, it become very easy for adolescents to see delinquency tolerance as normal. (7). Moral education as theory as postulated by Emile Durkhiem (1858-1917) helped to build the bridge between delinquency tolerance and socialization.

CHAPTER 7 REVIEW QUESTIONS

1. Define delinquency tolerance and discuss the concept in great detail.
2. How is self-restraint and self-concept relevant to delinquency tolerance?
3. How can you explain the age variable and delinquency tolerance with the data described in the chapters?

References

Akers, R. L. 1973 Deviant behavior: A social learning approach. Belmont, CA: Wadsworth Pub.

Albanese, I S. 1985 *Dealing with delinquency: An investigation of juvenile justice.* Lanham, MD: University Press of America.

Allan & Steffensmeier, 1988 . Sex disparities in arrests by residence, race and age: An assessment Of the gender consequence/ Crime; *Justice Quarterly,* 5:53-80.

Armand, C. 1891, Crime et suicide; etiologie generally; Factors individuals, sociologigues et cosmiques. Paris, 0. Doin

Ascheffenburg, G. 1913, Crime and its repression. Boston: Little, Brown and Company.

Barge, J. A. 1976 The status of selected Florida vocational education compensatory programs. Tallahassee, FL: Barge.

Barron, T. F., & Hartnage 1986 Labour marked experience and criminal behavior among Canadian youth: A longitudinal study. Department of Sociology, University of Alberta.

Becker, H. 1963 Outsiders: Studies in the sociology of deviance. 3rd ed. New York: Press.

Beckwith, J. 1976 "Social and political uses of genetics in the United States: Past and present." ed. by M. Lapp. New York: Annals of the New York Academy of Sciences.

Bohman, M. 1970 Adopted children and their families, a follow-up study of adopted children, their background, environment and adjustment. Stockholm, Proprius <Solna, Seelig>.

Boule, M. 1941 Fossil man, trans. by M. Bullock. New York: Drydere Press.

Buikhuisen, W. & Mednick, S. 1988 *Explaining criminal behavior: Interdisciplinary approaches.* Leiden, NY: E. J. Brill.

Chesney-Lind 1992 *Girls, delinquency, and juvenile justice*, 2nd ed. New York: Wadsworth Publishing Company.

Christiansen, K. 1977 A preliminary study of criminality among twins. In S. A. Mednick & K. 0. Christiansen (eds.). *Biosocial bases of criminal behavior* (pp. 89-108).

Cleckley, H. 1976 The mask of sanity: An attempt to clarify some issues about the so-called psychopathic personality, 5th ed. St. Louis: Mosby.

Cloward & Ohlin 1960 Delinquency and opportunity: A theory of delinquent gangs, an explanation of juvenile delinquency, focusing on differential opportunity.

Cohen, A. 1955 Delinquent Boys: *The culture of the gang.* A strain theoretical perspective on juvenile delinquency. New York: Free Press.

Cullen, F. T. 1983 *Rethinking crime and deviance theory: The emergence of a structuring tradition.* Totowa, NJ: Rowman & Allanheld.

Cusson, M. 1983 *Why delinquency?* Translated by D. R. Crelinstein. Toronto, Buffalo: University of Toronto Press.

Daly, K. 1989 "Gender and varieties of white-collar crime." *Criminology*, 27:769-793.

Deniker, J. 1926 The races of man: an outline of anthropology and ethnography. London: W. Scott Ltd., New York.

Durkheirn, E 1893 *The division of labor in society.* Translated by G. Simpson. New York: Free Press.

Eisner, V. 1969 *The delinquency label: The epidemiology of juvenile delinquency.* MA: Oxford Press.

Elliot, D., & Voss, H. *1974* Delinquency and dropout. Lexington, MA: Lexington Books.

Elliot, D., Ageton, Canter, Knowles, & Huizinga *1983* Theprevalenceand incidence of delinquent behavior *1976-1980:* National youth services. Report No. *26,* Boulder, CO: Behavioral Research Institute.

Ellis, L. *1982* Genetics and criminal behavior. *Criminology,* 20:43-66.

Empey, L. *1978American delinquency: Its meaning and construction.* Homewood, IL: Dorsey.

Eysenck, H. *1964 Crime andpersonality.* Boston: Houghton Mufflin.

Farnworth, T. *1984 Social* correla es of animal involvement: Further evidence of the relationship between social status and criminal behavior. *American Sociological Review, 47:505-518.*

Farrington, D. P. *1979,* Offending from 10 to 25 years of age.

Faust, F. L. *1970* Differential tolerance of delinquent behavior. Dissertation, Ohio.

Figueria-McDonough, J., & Selo, E. *1980* "A reformulation of the equal opportunity explanation of female delinquency." *Crime and Delinquency.26:333-343.*

Fishbein, D. H. *1990* "Biological perspectives in criminology." *Criminology, 28:27-72.*

Flowers, B. *1990* An examination of today's juvenile offenders (The adolescent criminal).

Frey, K. S. 1979 "Differential teaching methods used with girls and boys of moderate and high achievement levels." Paper presented at the annual meeting of the Society for Research in Child Development, San Francisco.

Galligan, C. 1982 *In a different voice: Psychological theory and women's development* Cambridge: Harvard University Press.

Garth, T. R.1950 *Race psychology: A study o f racial mental differences.* New York: Shittle Seyhouse, McGraw-Hill Book Company, Inc.

George, W. C. 1995 *The Biology of the Race Problem,* National Putnam Letters Committee.

Georges-Abeyie, D. 1984 "The criminal justice system and minorities: A review of literature." In Georges-Abeyie, D. (ed.), *Criminal justice system and blacks.* New York: Clark Boardman Company, Ltd.

Giordano, P., Cernkovich, S., & Pugh, M. D. 1985 "The missing cases in self-report delinquency research." *Journal of Criminal Law and Criminology, 76*(3):705-732.

Goddard, H. H. 1923 *Juvenile delinquency.* New York: Dodd, Mead.

Gould, L. C. 1981 Who defines delinquency: A comparison of self-reported and officially reported indices of delinquency for three racial groups. *Social Problems,* 16:325-336.

Gove, W. 1985 The effect of age and gender on deviant behavior: A biophysical perspective. In A. S. Rossi (ed.), *Gender and the Life Course (pp.* 115 144).

Henggler, S. 1989 *Delinquency in adolescence.* Newbury Park, CA: Sage.

Herrnstein, R. J., & Murray, C. 1994 *The Bell Curve: Intelligence and class structure in American life.* New York: Free Press.

Hindelang, M. J. 1971 "Age, sex, and the versatility of delinquent involvements." *Social Problems,* 18:522-535.

Hindelang, M. J. 1973 Causes of delinquency: A partial replication and extension. *Social Problems,* 20:471-487.

Hindelang, M. J. 1978 "Race and involvement in common law personal crimes." *American Sociological Review,* 43:93-109.

Hindelang, M. J. 1979 "Sex differences in criminal activity." *Social Problems,* 27:143-156.

Hirschi, T. 1969 *Cause of delinquency.* Berkeley: University of California Press.

Hirschi, T., & Gottsfredson, M. R. 1983 "Age and the explanation of crime." *American Journal ofSociology,* 89:552-584.

Hoyenga, K., & Hoyenga, K. T. 1979 *The question of sex differences: Psychological, cultural, and biological issues.* Boston: Little, Brown.

Huizinga, D., & Elliot, D. S. 1987 "Juvenile offenders: Prevalence, offender incidence and arrest rates by race." *Crime and Delinquency,* 3 3:206-223.

Hylton, M. O., & Finn, P. 1994Using civil remedies for criminal behavior: Rationale, case studies, and constitutional issues.

Jenkins, R. 1955 "Adaptive and maladaptive delinquency." *The Nervous Child,* 11:9-11, in DD2C (69).

Jensen, G., & Eve, R. 1976 Sex differences in delinquency: An examination of popular sociological explanations. *Criminology,* 12:427-448.

John, A., & Gibbons, D. 1987Age patterns in criminal involvement. *International Journal of Offender Therapy and Comparative Criminology,* 31:237-260.

Kitsuse, J., & Dietrick, C. D. 1959 "Societal reaction to deviant behavior: Problems of theory and method." *Social Problems,* 9:247-256.

Kreur, P. D., & Rose, H. M. 1972 *Race, place, and risk.- Black homicide in urban America.* Albany, NY: State University of New York Press.

Lander, B. 1954*Towards an understanding of juvenile delinquency.* New York: Columbia University Press.

Leonard, E. B. 1982*Women, crime and society: A critique of criminological theory.* New York: Longman.

Leonard, E., & Sontheimer, H. 1995 *Juvenile court and sentencing disparities,* 1 st ed. New York: Longman.

Locke, J. 1952*Epistola de tolerantia: A letter concerning toleration.* Chicago: Encyclopedia Britannica.

Loeb, K., & Mednick, S. A. 1977 *Biological bases of criminal behavior.* New York: Gardner Press.

Lohman, J. D. 1979*A study of juvenile delinquency: The police and the community.* Washington, DC: Supt. of Docs., U.S.G.P.O.

Louis Harris & Associates, 1982 . *The myth and reality of aging in America*. Washington, DC: National Council on the Aging.

Luscri, G. 1995"Dealing with family disfunction." In *Contemporary Issues, African Times*. Lagos: University of Lagos Press.

Lynch, M. J. 2000. J. Phillippe Rushton on Crime: An Examination and Critique of the Explanation of Crime in 'Race, Evolution and Behavior.' Social Pathology. 6,3: 228-244.

Lynch, M. J., R. J. Michalowski, and W. B. Groves. 2000. The New Primer in Radical Ciminology. Monsey, New York: Criminal Justice Press.

Maccoby, E., & Jacklin, J. P. 1969 "Community integration and the social control of juvenile delinquency." *Journal of Social Issues,* 14:38-51.

Mann, C. R. 1986 "Race and sentencing of women felons: Percentage of crime index arrests by race," *International Journal of Women Studies,* 7(2):160-172.

Mann, C. R. 1993 *Unequal justice: A question of color.* Bloomington & Indianapolis, IN: Indiana University Press.

Mattick, H. W. 1979*Criminology: New concerns: Essays in honor of Hans W. Mattick.*

Matza, D. 1964 *Delinquency and Drift*. New York: Wiley.

McCord, W.1968 "Delinquency: Psychological aspects" (pp. 86-93. In D. L. Sills (ed.) *International Encyclopedia of Social Sciences, vol. 4,* New York: Macmillan/Free Press.

McCord, J., & McCord, W. 1956 *Psychopathy and delinquency.* New York: Macmillan Free Press.

McCord, J., & McCord, W. 1959 *Origins of crime: A new evaluation of the Cambridge-Somerville youth study.* New York: Columbia University Press.

McGahey, R. 1986 .*Economic conditions, neighborhood organization, and urban crime,* A. Reiss & M. Tonry (eds). Chicago: University of Chicago Press.

McGuire, W. 1979 *Current topics.* New York: Plenum Press.

McNeely & Pope 1978. "Race and involvement in common law personal crime: A response to Hindelang." *The Review of Black Political Economy,* 8:405-410.

Mednick, A. & Moffit, J. T. 1986 *Biological contributions to crime causation.* Beverly Hills, CA: Sage.

Merton, R. 1938 Social structure and anomie. *American Sociological Review,* 31:672-682.

Messerschmidt, J. W. 1986 *Capitalism, patriarchy, and crime: Toward a socialist feminist criminology.* Totowa, JN: Rowan and Littlefield.

Miller, W. B. 1958 "Inter-institutional conflict as a major impediment to delinquency prevention." *Human Organization,* 10: 168-19 1.

Mills, J. S. 1892 On liberty. London: Longmans, Green.

Milton, J., & Yinger, R. 1994 *Ethnicity: Source of strength? Source of conflict?* Washington, DC: Free Press.

Morash, M. 1984 "Establishment of a juvenile police record: The influence of individual and peer group characteristics." *Criminology,* 22:97-111.

Nunn, C. Z., Crockett, H. J., & Williams, J. A. 1978 Tolerance for nonconformity. San Francisco: Jossey-Bass Publishers.

Nye, F. I. 195 8 *Family relationships and delinquent behavior.* New York: Wiley.

Nye, F. I., Short, J. F., & Olson, V. J. 1958 Social economic status and delinquent behavior. *American Journal of Sociology,* 63:381-389.

Olweus, D., Matlsson, A, Scholling, D., & Low, H. 1980 "Testosterone, aggression, physical and personality dimensions in normal adolescent males." *Psychosomatic Medicine,* 42:2 5 3 -269.

Paternoster, R. 1978The labeling effects of police apprehension: Identity, exclusion, and secondary deviance. Thesis: Florida State University.

Phelps, T. R. 1976 *Juvenile delinquency: A contemporary view.* Pacific Palisades, CA: Goodyear Pub. Co.

Piaget, J. 1932 *The moral judgement of the child*. London: Kegan Paul.

Pope, C. E.; Feyerhenn, W. H.; & Leonard, K. K. 1995Minorities in the juvenile justice system: Research summers: U.S. Dept. of Justice, Office of Justice Programs. California: Sage Pub. Inc.

Quetelet, A. 1969 A treatise on man and the development of his faculties. A fascism. Reproduction of the English translation of 1842.

Raine, A. 1993 *The psychopathology of crime: Criminal behavior as a clinical disorder*. San Diego, CA: Academic Press.

Rankin, J. H. 1980 "Changing attitudes toward capital punishment." *Social Forces*, 58:194211.

Reckless, W. C. R. 1961 *The Crime Problem*. New York: Appleton-Century.

Reckless, W. C. 1970 "Self-concept as an indicator against delinquency." In J. E. Teele (ed.), *Juvenile delinquency: A leader*. Itasca, IL: Peacock.

Reitzes, A. 1951 "Delinquency as the failure of personal and social controls." *American Sociological Review*, 16:196-207.

Robbins, L. N. 1966 *Deviant children grown up*. New York: Human Sciences Press.

Rotter, J. B. 1971 External and internal control. *Psychology Today*, 5:37.

Rowe, A. 1986 Genetic and envirom-nental components of anti-social behavior. *Criminology*, 24:513-532.

Rowe, A., & Tittle, C.1977 "Life cycle changes and criminal propensity." *Sociological Quarterly*, 18:223-236.

Sampson, R. J., & Laub, J. H. 1990 "Unemployment, marital discord, and deviant behavior: The long-term correlates of childhood misbehavior." *American Society of Criminology*.

Sandberg, D. N. 1985 "The abuse-delinquency connection and juvenile court responsibility." *Justice for children*, 1: 10- 11.

Schur, E. M. 1974 *Radical nonintervention: Rethinking delinquency problem*. Englewood Cliffs, NJ: Prentice-Hall.

Schwartz, J. M.; Guo, P.; & Kerbs, C. 1992 *Public attitudes toward juvenile crime andjuvenile justice: Implicationfor public policy.* Ann Arbor: University of Michigan Press.

Sellin, T. 1964 *Culture, conflict and crime.* New York: Social Science Research Council,

Sharp, P. M. 1983 Tolerance of delinquency: "A study of juveniles in a small town. Oklahoma City: University Press.

Shaw, C., & McKay, H. 1932 Social factors in juvenile delinquency. A publication of the national Commission on Law Observance and Enforcement, No. 13, vol. 2, 6/26.

Shelley, J. F. 1995 *Criminology: A contemporary handbook,* 2nd ed. Wadsworth Publishing Company.

Shoemaker, D. J. 1984 *Theories ofdelinquency: An examination of explanations of delinquent* & 1990 *behavior.* New York: Oxford University Press.

Short, J. 1964" Gang delinquency and anomie." In B. Marshall & B. Clinard (eds.), *Anomie and deviant behavior.* Chicago: University of Chicago Press.

Simmons, R. L., & Blyth, D. 1987 *Moving into adolescence: The impact of pubertal change and social context.* New York: Aldine de Gruyter.

Smith, M. D., & Preston, V. 1977 "Gender and crime." *American Sociological Review,* 48:509-514.

Spohn, C.; Cassia, S.; Gruhl, J.; & Welch, S. 1982 "The effect of race on sentencing: A re-examination on an unsettled question." *Law and Society Review,* 16:71-88.

Spohn, C.; Walker, S.; & Delone, M. 1996 *The color ofjustice: Race, ethnicity, and crime in America.* Belmont, CA: Wadsworth Pub. Co.

Steffensmeier, D. 1980"Sex differences in patterns of adult crime, 1965-1977." *Social Forces,* 58:1080-1109.

Steffensmeier, D., & Allen, E. 1988 "Sex disparities in arrests by residence, race, and age: An assessment of gender convergence/crime hypothesis." *Justice Quarterly,* 5:53-80.

Steffensmeier, D.; Allan, E.; & Streifel, C. 1989"Development and female crime: A cross-national test of alternative explanations." *Social Forces*, 68.

Suttles, G. 1968 *The social order of the slum*. Chicago: University of Chicago Press.

Sykes, G., & Matza, D. 1957 "Techniques of neutralization: A theory of delinquency." *American Sociological Review*, 22:664-670.

Tannenbaum, F. 1936 *Crime and the community*. New York: Columbia University Press.

Tappan, P. 1949 *Juvenile delinquency*. New York: McGraw-Hill.

Taylor, C. S., et al. 1993 *Girls, gangs, women and drugs*. East Lansing, MI: Michigan State University Press.

Tinder, G. 1976 Tolerance: Toward a new civility. Amherst: University of Massachusetts Press.

Trojanowicz, R.1973 Juvenile delinquency: Concepts and control. Washington, DC: National Institute of Justice.

Vold, G., & Bernard, T. J. 1986 Theoretical criminology, 3rd ed. New York: Oxford University Press.

Warr, M. 1993 "Age, peers, and delinquency." *Criminology*, 31:17-40.

Webster's Dictionary 1983 Simon Schuster, Prentice-Hall.

Weigel, S.; Vernon, D. H.; & Tognacci, V. 1965 *The psychological responses of children*. Springfield, IL: C. C. Thomas & 1974

Werthman, M. L. 1963"Delinquency in Schools," *Journal of Sociology* (vol.8, 39-60).

Winslow, R. W. 1963 *Juvenile Delinquency in a Free Society*. New York: Free Press.

Wolfgang, M., & Ferracati, F. 1967 *The subculture of violence: Towards an integrated theory in criminology*. Beverly Hills, CA: Sage.

Wolfgang, M., Figlio, R. M., & Sellin, T. 1972 *Delinquency in a birth cohort*. Chicago: University of Chicago Press.

Wolfgang, M., Thomberry, T., & Figlio, R. 1987 *From boy to man, from delinquency to crime.* Chicago: University of Chicago Press.

Yeudall, Z. A. 1977 *The brain's impact on behavior.* Canada: Elsevier Science Pub. Co.

Zimring, R. 1981. Kids, groups and crime: Some implications of well-known secrets. *Journal of Criminal Law and Criminology,* 72:867-885.

Revised Code of Washington, *The Juvenile Justice Act,* 1994, Title 13.

About the Author

Evaristus Obinyan received a Bachelor's degree in Liberal Arts and Science with criminal justice emphasis from the University of Illinois at Chicago in 1988 and a Master of Science degree in Corrections and Criminal Justice from the Chicago State University in 1989. He began a Ph.D program in Criminology at Florida State University in fall of 1989. Due to some unfortunate spasmodic conjugation and or ticklings he was forced to find full time employment that took him to work at the Texas department of criminal justice institutional division. He returned to complete the doctoral program at Florida State University in 1997 to no avail. During this time, he began work as adjunct instructor at Florida A and M University until the year 2000 when he landed a full time Assistant Professor teaching job at Benedict college in Columbia, South Carolina. The Florida State University experience was a painful lesson and it taught Evaristus that giving up was not an option.

Evaristus began studies in the department of Criminology at the University of South Florida in Tampa, Florida while teaching at Fort Valley State University. He was also named the Director of the newly established Georgia Center for Juvenile Justice at the university. The Center was opened primarily to evaluate the juvenile crime particularly disproportionate minority contact and confinement and make recommendation to state agencies and juvenile community-based programs. This effort brought about one of the large- scale project- disproportionate minority contact and confinement in two counties, Peach and Crawford due for publication. Evaristus was lead investigator in that project. He has also made several academic presentations at regional, national and international meetings. His review of Pyongyang, The North Korea Capital can be found in the Journal of Asia and African Studies. More of his articles are due for publication in 2005.